Introduction by the Hon. Harriet Cotterell

As a self-taught home dressmaker, for many years I had battled with bought patterns, trying to alter them to my size and the exact style I wished to achieve. For though I was never 'stock' size for ready-made clothes neither was I 'stock' size for patterns. And then too I found different makes of patterns worked out larger or smaller than the supposed size. However by dint of a lot of work I usually managed to make a wearable garment in the material and approximate style that I wanted — even if I was left with extra material as the bought pattern always overstated the necessary yardage! But these garments which I made with such care were never perfect and I never felt really happy wearing them.

One day I heard of Mr. Benjamin and his revolutionary method of design and cutting. I was greatly excited and immediately wrote to Mr. Benjamin, who kindly invited me down to Brighton to attend a class so that I could see for myself how simple, direct and different his method is. When I entered the room where the fifth lesson was in progress, the first thing that struck me was the wide range of people attending the class all, as I later learnt for a variety of different reasons. There was a mother with school-age children; a mother with a todler; a young designer, who could design admirably but was not good at cutting out his designs; an old-age pensioner who said that only by making her clothes could she afford to clothe herself, but though she had never made anything before she found it very easy; a pretty young housewife who liked to wear fashionable clothes that really fitted her. These people and others who attended the class were unanimous in saying how easy and pleasurable they found dress-cutting and making with Mr. Benjamin's method as it involved no complicated learning, mathematics or any rigmarole, and that they had without exception found it not only possible but enjoyable making a garment of their choice of design and material for the very first time.

Yet many of these people had tried books on dress-making, patterns etc. with dismal results, so what was Mr. Benjamin's secret? I sat watching and listening to what was, in fact, the Fifth Lesson. Having taken their individual body measurements, they now marked those required onto brown paper, according to the brief and clear instructions written by Mr. Benjamin (which were accompanied by a clear diagram) drew in the requisite lines and commenced cutting their patterns. All this in less than an hour! Afterwards they used the pattern to arrange the best and most economical lay-out with regard to the material, and then cut their design out of the material.

Because Mr. Benjamin's instructions are brief and uncomplicated, and the diagrams explicit and clear, the students are able to continue working at home. I saw some dresses which had been made as a result of the Fifth Lesson, and the students were kind enough to put them on to show me how perfectly they fitted. I was deeply impressed by the cut and fit of the dresses, and by the individual styles.

Also, as one of them said, it was marvellous to be able to choose absolutely the right material and without waste of money or effort convert this quickly into a desirable garment.

Mr. Benjamin also teaches one how to interpret a made-up garment back into a pattern: one mother told how she had seen a little boy's party shirt and shorts in a shop, made a rough sketch on a scrap of paper and then rushed home to make a pattern. She then produced the finished shirt and shorts, which were beautifully made in every respect with some delightful detailing.

I learnt a very great deal from observing just this one lesson, and I look forward to the publication of Mr. Benjamin's book so that, purely selfishly, I may make myself some well-cut trousers, and more generously, so that others may share the happiness of easy and superb dress-cutting and making.

Harriet Cotterell.

Dear Reader,

As Lecturer at Colleges of Cutting and Design, I have always felt there was a great need for a book of this nature — a very simplified method of Cut and Design, breaking through the 'mystique' which has previously surrounded this profession.

The purpose of this book is to cater for people who would like to copy or create their own designs and cut patterns to any size they wish, yet not have the worry of learning how.

My simple instructions show how to cut your Master Block, which is kept permanently. This is cut from a thick paper or preferably card-board as it is used to trace new patterns each time a new style of dress is cut.

With most methods of Pattern Cutting and Designing, a wide knowledge of mathematics is presupposed. It has always been my aim to simplify the entire process so that it is completely clear to both novice and practised dressmaker alike.

By the time this book has been read you will be amazed to find that you can cut and design the most beautiful clothes — dresses, suits, coats and trousers.

I am happy that this book has now been completed and hope you derive much pleasure from its pages and that it will be of great value to you both now and in the future.

Sincerely,

J. Benjamin

PRINCIPAL

New Method of Cut and Design
(Inc. West London Garment Cutting Academy)

Sally Grantham 4.50
London May 80

THE MODERN DRESSMAKER

THE
MODERN DRESSMAKER

by

J. Benjamin

Published by J. Benjamin, Flag Court, Hove, Sussex.

© J. Benjamin (New Method Cut & Design) 1972

Enlarged edition 1979

ISBN 0 9502576 1-3

All rights reserved. No part of this publication may be reproduced, stored in a retrieval system, or transmitted in any form or by any means, electronic, mechanical, photocopying, recording or otherwise, without prior permission of the publisher.

Cover photographs by Photo Life, Alfriston, Sussex.
Printed by Island Press Seaford, Seaford, Sussex.

Contents

Page	Part	
9		Equipment Necessary for Design and Cutting.
11	1	Measuring Correctly.
13	2	Block for Back of Dress.
15	3	Block for Front of Dress.
17	4	One Piece Sleeve.
19	5	Underarm Bust Darts.
21	6	Shoulder Darts.
23	7	Back Darts.
25	8	Skirt Back Block.
27	9	Skirts with Knife Pleats, Inverted or Box Pleats.
29	10	Flaired Two Piece Skirt.
31	11	Roll and Standing Collars.
33	12	Shirt Collar.
35	13	Peter Pan Collar.
37	14	Back Block for Tailored Jacket or Coat.
39	15	Front Block for Tailored Jacket or Coat.
41	16	Two Piece Sleeve for Tailored Jacket or Coat.
43	17	Under Collar for Tailored Jacket or Coat.
45		Garments requiring Facings.
47	18	Front Block for Trousers.
49	19	Back Block for Trousers.
51	20	Two Piece Raglan Sleeve.
53	21	Round Back Figure.
55	22	Leaving Inlays.
57	23	Dress Design A.
59	24	Transferring Design A to Pattern.
61	25	Transferring Design A to Pattern cont.
63	26	Pattern Lay for Dress Design A.
65	27	Blazer Styles Single and Double Breasted.
67	28	Double or Single Breasted Blazers.
69	29	Draping for The Beginner.
70	30	Block Pattern for Childrens Dresses
73	31	Cutting a Dress to Your Own Design
74	32	Dress A
76	33	Dress B
78	34	Block Pattern for Girls and Boys Coats
81	35	Mark Stitching
83	36	Skirt Making
89	37	Making a Dress
91	38	Trouser Making
93	39	Jacket and Coat Making
95	40	Cutting Facings and Collars
97	41	Pocket Making
113	42	Button Holes
117	43	Altering Clothes to Fit
121	44	Garments that Twist at Back of Arm Holes
123	45	Garments that Twist in Front of Arm Holes
125	46	Clothes that are too tight
127	47	How to make a Skirt from your Slax without using a Pattern
129	48	Making a Sleeve Length Poncho without using a Pattern
131	49	Relining Skirt without using a Pattern
133	50	Fly Fronts for Slax
135	51	Trouser Side Pockets
137	52	Using an Old Pattern for a Changed Figure
141	53	Cutting a Waistcoat and Skirt without a paper Pattern
145	54	Cutting Checked or Striped Materials
147	55	Cutting and Making a Tiered Skirt without using a Pattern
153	56	The Tabard
155	57	The Pinafore Dress
161	58	Over Dress
165	59	Smocked Tops
168	60	Cutting Velvet or Materials with a Pile

Metric Conversion

1/4	6mm
3/8	9mm
1/2	13mm
5/8	16mm
3/4	19mm
7/8	22mm
1"	25mm
2"	50mm
3"	76mm
4"	102mm
5"	127mm
6"	152mm
7"	178mm
8"	203mm
9"	229mm
10"	254mm
11"	279mm
12"	305mm
24"	610mm
36"	914mm

Equipment Necessary for Designing and Cutting

Drawing Pencil
Pencil Sharpener
Tracing Wheel
Brown or White Cutting Paper
Calico or cheap Cotton can be used for making skeleton fittings.

Ruler — This may be of metal, wood, or perspex and should be 18" long.

Tailor's Set-Square — This is a plate of wood in the form of a right-angled triangle with one side left open, the angle formed being 45°. One arm is 24" in length, the other 12".

The Tailors set-square is used when designing the pattern or block as a guide for drawing lines. One edge of the set-square is placed parallel with the edge of pattern paper, the other therefore runs horizontally across the pattern paper. All lines can therefore be measured accurately to give correct balance.

Tape Measure — This must be of the type which does not stretch and has brass ends. Ensuring reliability in use.

Chalk — Light and dark coloured non-waxy Tailor's chalk is necessary for marking through and around the block onto the fabric all the desired markings. It is also used for adjustments when fitting a garment.

Cutting or Dressmaker's Shears — This should be 7" to 8" long and is essential for good clean cutting lines.

Pinking Shears — Scissors with zig-zag interlocking blades again 7" to 8" long. The raw edges of many synthetic fabrics are liable to fray, and it is useful to pink these. Very thick fabrics need pinking along the seams to avoid bulkiness and make the seams lie flatter.

Measuring Correctly

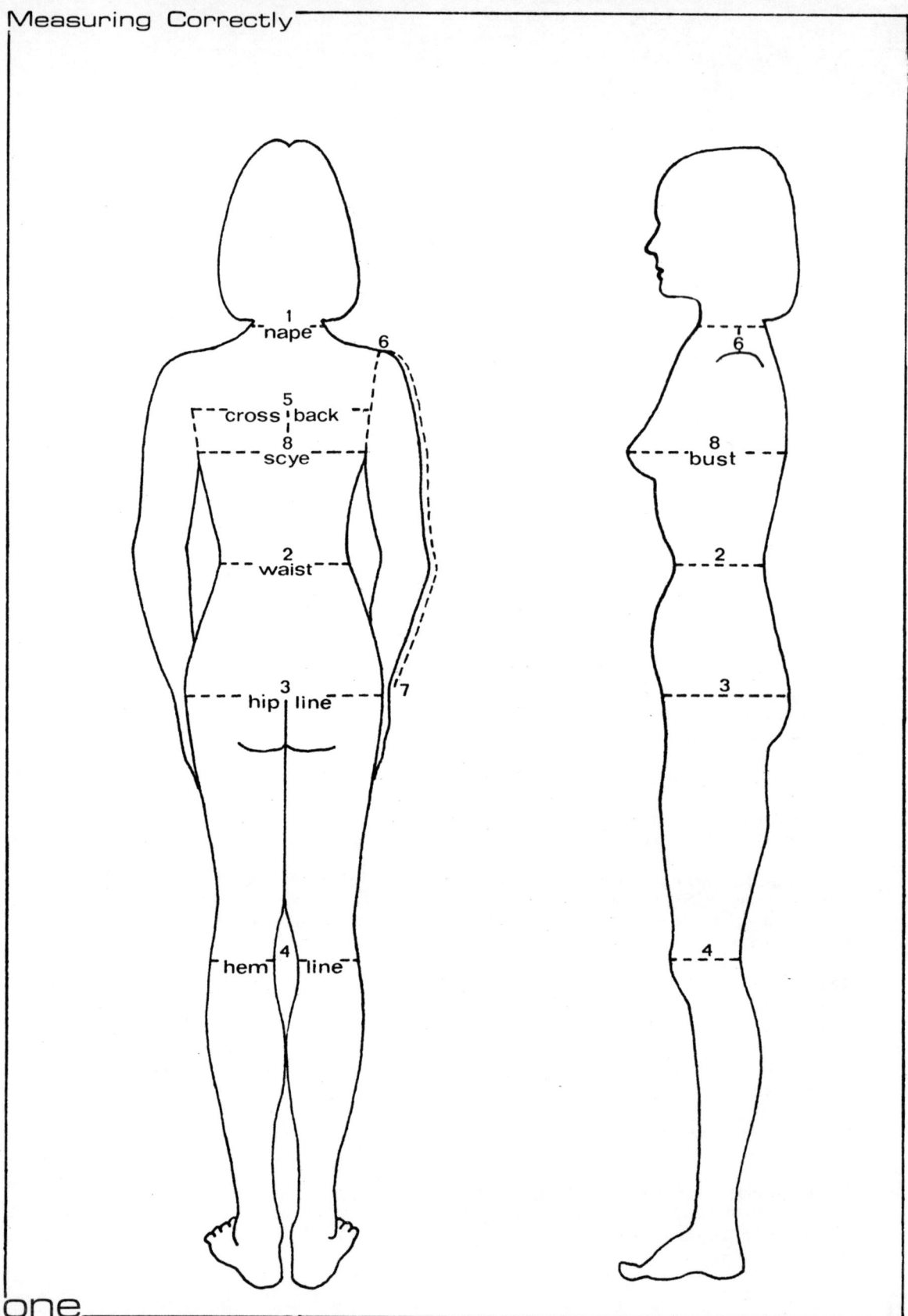

one

Measuring Correctly

It is very important that measurements are taken correctly. The following is a very simple and accurate method.

1 at nape of neck to 2 is waist length.

1 at nape of neck to 3 is hip length.

1 at nape of neck to 4 is full length of dress.

5 is half cross back measure taken from centre back to armhole.

6 is sleeve length taken from armhole shoulder at 6 to required length plus $\frac{3}{8}$" for seam at 7.

8 is bust measurement. Place tape around back coming as close as possible to under armhole (scye line at 8) across to most prominent part of bust. Do not hold tape tight. It is advisable to keep two fingers inside of tape measure as this will assure extra ease.

Waist measurement is taken at line 2 (waist line). Always add 2" to allow for movement and ease.

Hip measurement should always be taken at most prominent part of hips as line 3 shows.

From these measurements you will now be able to cut your block pattern.

When taking measurements for a skirt: first take your length, next your waist measurement — this should be taken net as you will always allow extra on your pattern for back darts. Your next measurement is your hips — taken the same way as for your dress. These are the only three measurements required for a skirt.

Block for Back of Dress

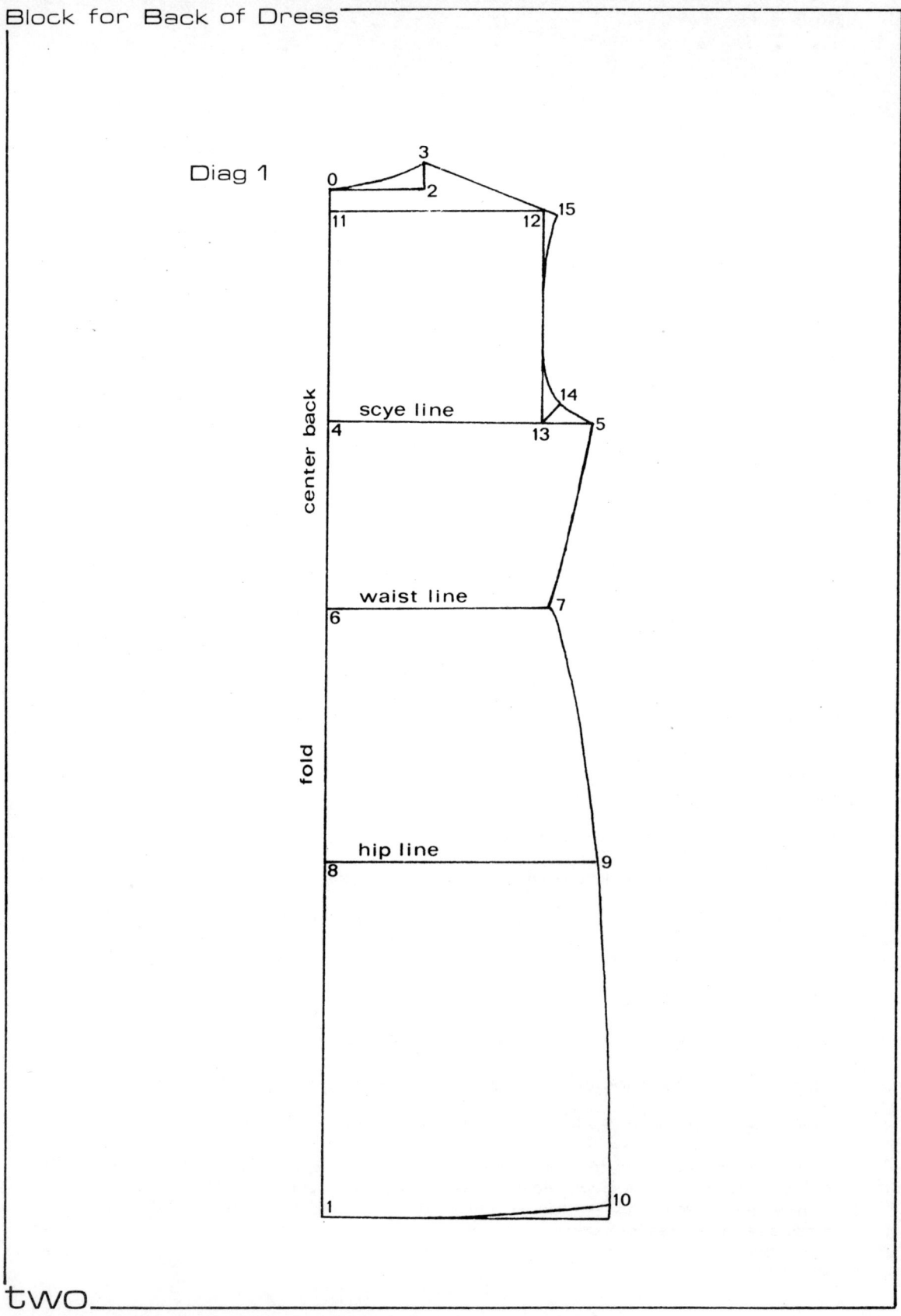

Diag 1

two

Block for Back of Dress

By using the following instructions you can cut your block to any required size.

Your first step is to get your scale, as this is your guide to certain points of the garment.

To obtain your scale you take $\frac{1}{3}$ of your bust measurement **plus 6''**. For example to get scale for 36'' bust — $\frac{1}{3}$'' of 36'' = 12'' + 6'' = 18''. Therefore your scale is 18 for a 36'' bust and over. For measurements under 36'' bust you take **half** your bust measurement and this becomes your scale.

Measurements I have used for this block are:

Nape of neck to waist 16''
Nape of neck to hips 24''
Nape of neck to full length 36''
Half cross back 7''
Sleeve length 22''
Bust 36''
Waist 28''
Hips 38''

Scale 18 for Diag 1

0 to 1 equals full length of dress. This is cut on fold of paper as diagram shows being centre back of garment.

0 to 2 equals $\frac{1}{6}$ **of scale** this is 3'' (being a $\frac{1}{6}$ of 18).

3 is ¾'' from shoulder points. This measurement is always the same for all sizes.

Shape neck from 0 to 3. This is your back neck line.

0 to 4 is half scale minus ½'' for scye line.

4 to 5 is ¼ bust measurement plus ½'' for seams and ease. This is your scye line as shown on the measure chart.

6 is waist line (16'' from nape).

6 to 7 is ¼ waist measurement + ½'' for seams and ease.

8 is hip line (24'' from nape).

8 to 9 is ¼ hip measurement + ½'' for seams and ease.

Draw side seam line through 5-7 to 10. 10 being ½'' up from line squared out from 1. This to be about ½'' wider than 9 or any required width for bottom of dress.

11 is 1½'' from 0.

12 is squared out from 11 which is a half of the cross back measurement + ½'' for seams and ease.

13 is squared down from 12 on to scye line.

14 is ¾'' from 13.

15 is ¼'' out from 12 for shoulder line.

Shape shoulder and armhole running **straight** line from 3 to 15 and **rounded** line from 15 to 14 and on to 5.   Your back block is now complete.

Block for Front of Dress

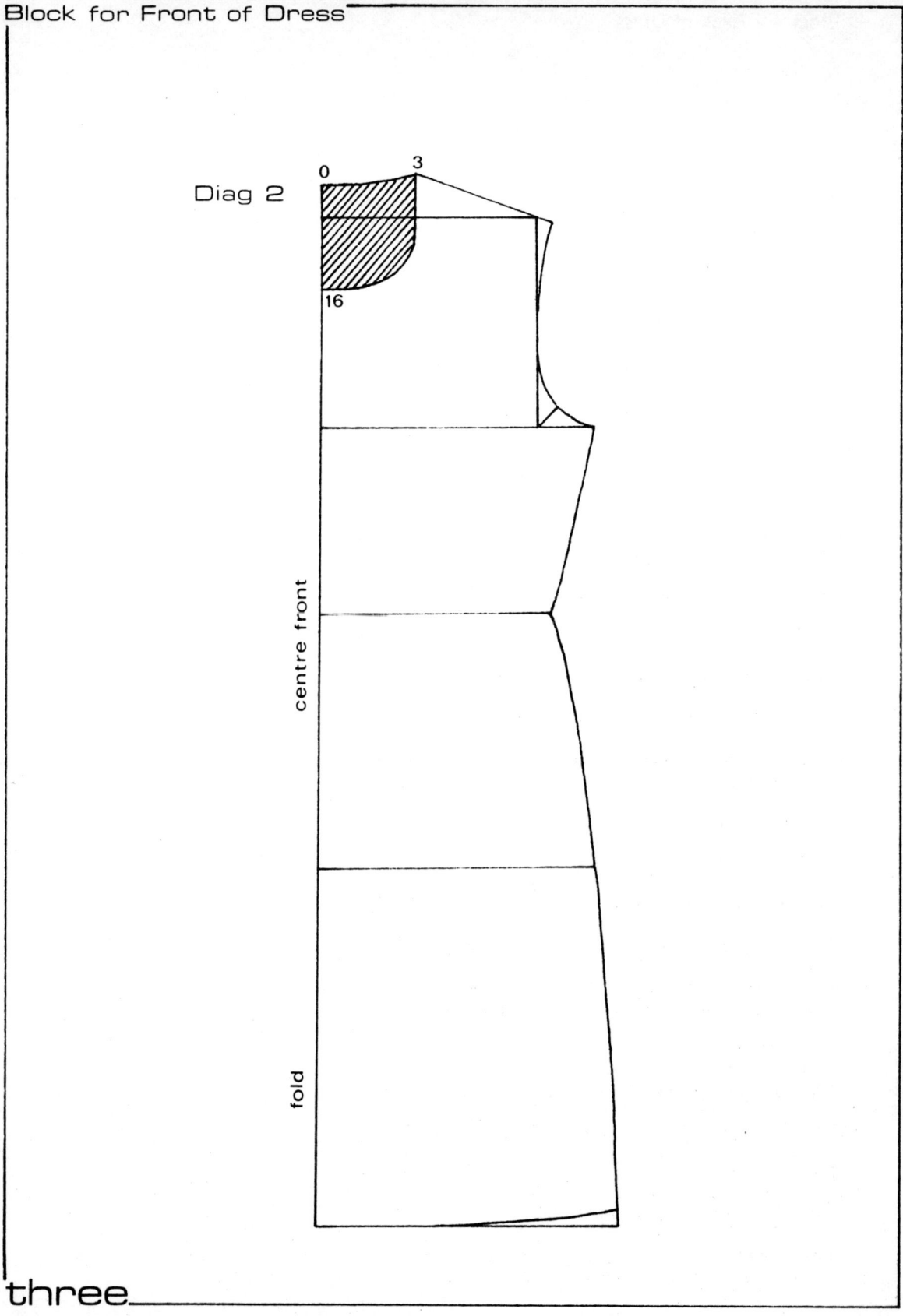

Diag 2

three

Block for Front of Dress

The front block of your dress is cut identically to your back block pattern using the same measurements and can be cut by laying your back block on to the cutting paper and marking it out. The only adjustment is the shaping of the neck.

For a round neck 0 to 16 is 3" this can be raised or lowered to any required position. 3" is a good average. You can also cut a square neck or any other style you choose to shape.

This completes your back and front block pattern.

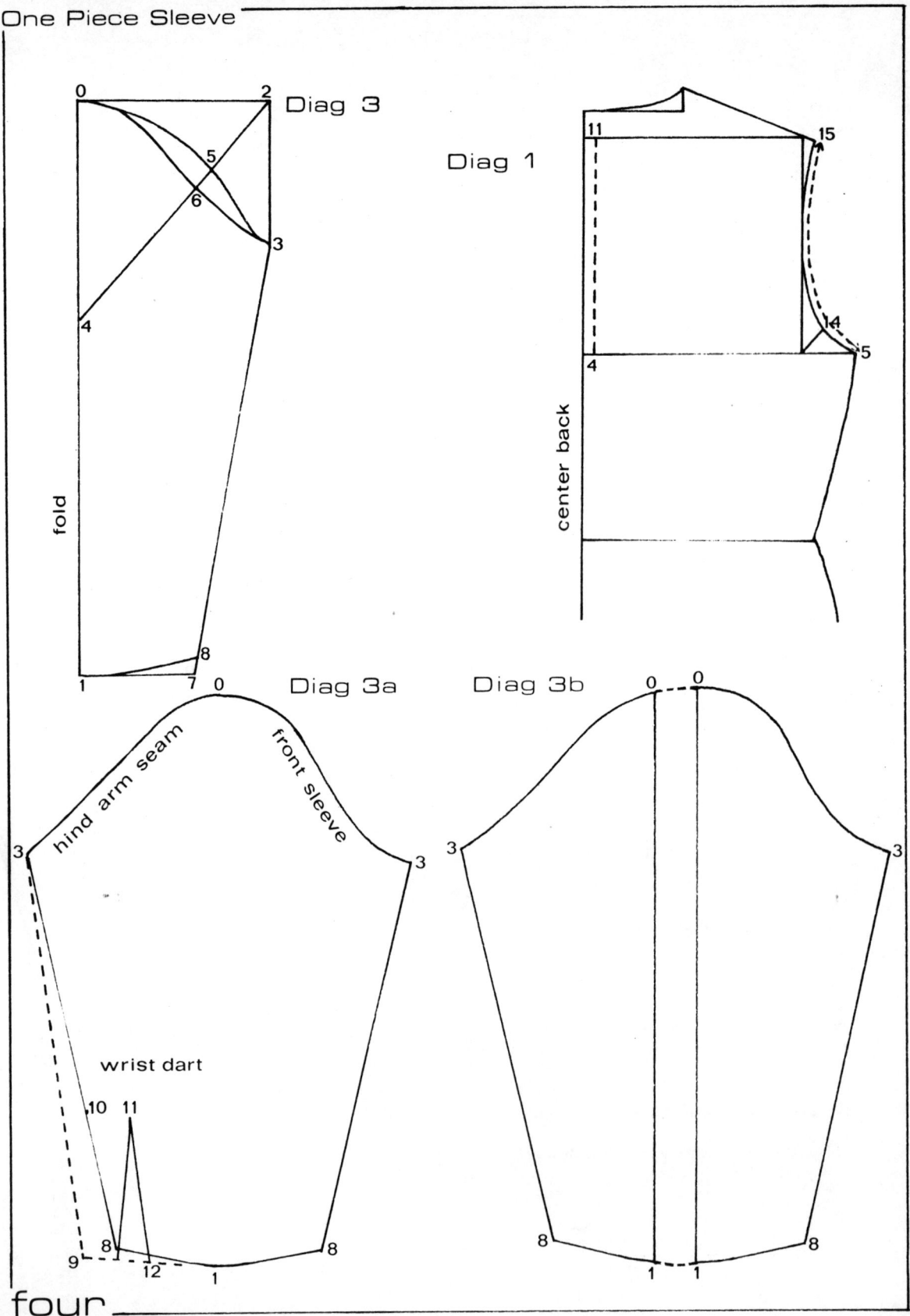

One Piece Sleeve

Diag 3

0 to 1 is full length of sleeve plus $\frac{3}{8}$" for seams. This is cut on fold of paper.

2 from 0 is same distance as back armhole of block pattern at 5-14 on to 15 minus ½". Broken line on diagram 1 indicates where to measure.

3 from 2 of sleeve is distance of 11 to 4 on the back block minus ¾" as shown by broken line on centre back.

4 from 0 is 9½" run line from 2 to 4.

5 from 2 is 3½".

6 from 5 is ¾".

7 is squared out from 1 Diag 3 to any width of cuff you wish, average is 4¾"

Shape line from 3 to 5 on to 0 as indicated, this is your hindarm sleeve head. Note shaping of sleeve coming in slightly at 3. Now run line from 3 to 6 on to 0 for forearm sleeve head.
When opened out you have a one piece sleeve complete. Should you require an easy sleeve yet well fitted at the wrist, a wrist dart is recommended, instructions as follows:

Diag 3a

9 is 1½" squared out from 8.

Broken lines from 3 to 9 and on to 1 are your new cutting lines.

10 from 8 is half way between 3 and 8 minus 1".

8 from 7 is 1".

11 is 2" from 10.

12 is 1½" from 8.

Run line from 8 to 11 and from 12 to 11.

This completes your wrist dart. This dart can be adjusted for positioning either backward or forward according to one's elbow. This can best be done when fitting on dress and pinning to required position.
The one piece sleeve pattern can be used for several different styles by simple adjustment. Here are a few examples:

Diag 3b

For a **Puffed Sleeve** you cut through your sleeve pattern from 0 to 1, lay your two pieces side by side about 3" to 4" apart depending on how full you want the sleeves, then cut as **one piece.** You now have the extra amount for easing in. Sleeves should be cut approximately 3" longer than required length to allow for full puff.

A very practical way of making up this style of sleeve is to cut a separate pair of sleeves using net or fine interlining. These are cut the same size and length as your block patterns. You now sew up **separately** all the four front seams through 3 to 8. Now take one net and one of your sleeves, sew them together through 3-5-6-0 and all through sleeve head by easing in sleeve to size of net sleeve. The cuff is then sewn by easing in sleeve to net. As the net is cut shorter than the sleeve you will find this gives a well styled puffed sleeve, this should now be ready for sewing into your dress.

For a wide sleeve guaged in at the cuff, cut your sleeve head around numbers 0-3-5-6 in the normal way, and simply **add width** at cuff to any required size, from **8 to nothing at 3.** You then cut your cuff band to any length and width you wish and ease in surplus of sleeve into cuff band.

By using this method there are many styles of sleeve you will be able to cut, but always be certain that when your sleeve is complete it must be the same size as your block pattern around sleeve head at numbers 3-5-6-0, otherwise you may find the sleeve will not fit correctly into the armhole of your dress.

Underarm Bust Darts

Diag 4

five

Underarm Bust Darts

Underarm darts are sometimes used in preference to shoulder darts, depending on design of dress or prominence of bust. Either of these darts will avoid underarm wrinkles.

Diag 4

A is 4½" from 5 which is the bust line.

B is ¾" from 5.

C is ¾" from 5.

Run line from B to A and C to A. This is your dart.

Broken line D is 1½" up from 5 for new armhole.

E is 1½" up from 15 for new shoulder line.

Curve side seam from B to D coming out ¼" as shown by broken line.

These adjustments are required to replace quantity taken in at darts. If it is necessary to take a deeper dart, extra allowances should be made at armhole and shoulder.

Shoulder Darts

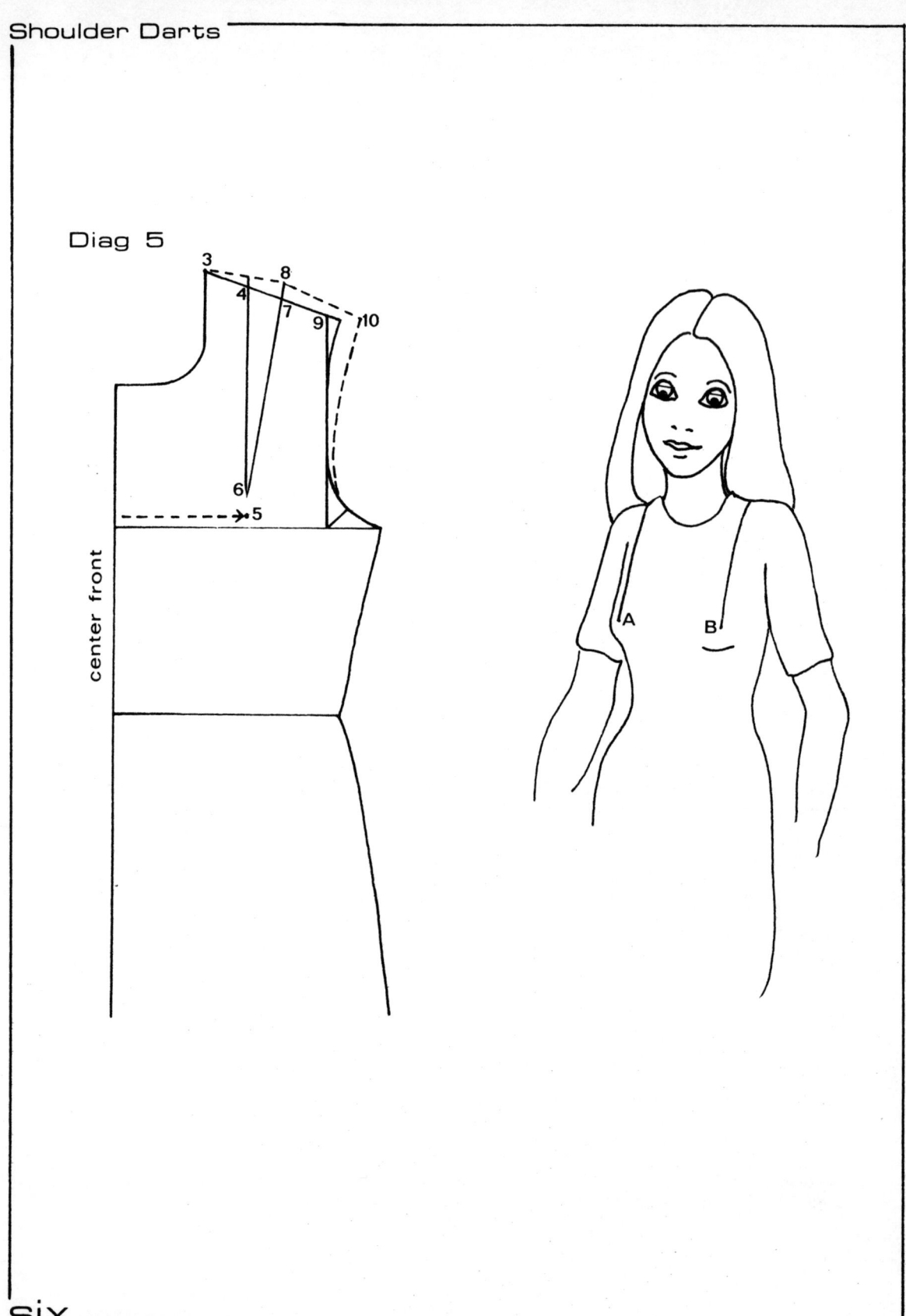

Diag 5

six

Shoulder Darts

Shoulder darts are cut to give fulness and ease at most prominent part of bust and should finish 1″ above bust points.

Diag 5

Broken line at shoulder and armhole is allowance for quantity taken in at darts.

Darts should not be cut through but only tacked up for fitting so that they can be adjusted if necessary.

Sometimes a deeper dart is required between 4 and 7. To allow for this an extra 1″ can be added at armhole, from 10 down to bottom of broken line.

4 is 1½″ from 3.

5 from centre front is half distance between bust points A and B on drawing.

6 is 1″ up from 5.

Run line from 4 to 6.

7 is 2″ from 4.

8 from 6 is same distance as 4 to 6 running through 7.

10 is extended from 9 the same distance as 4 to 7, this is 2″.

Broken line is run from 3-8-10 coming in at bottom of armhole corresponding with end of dart at 6. This is your new shoulder and armhole cutting line.

Back Darts

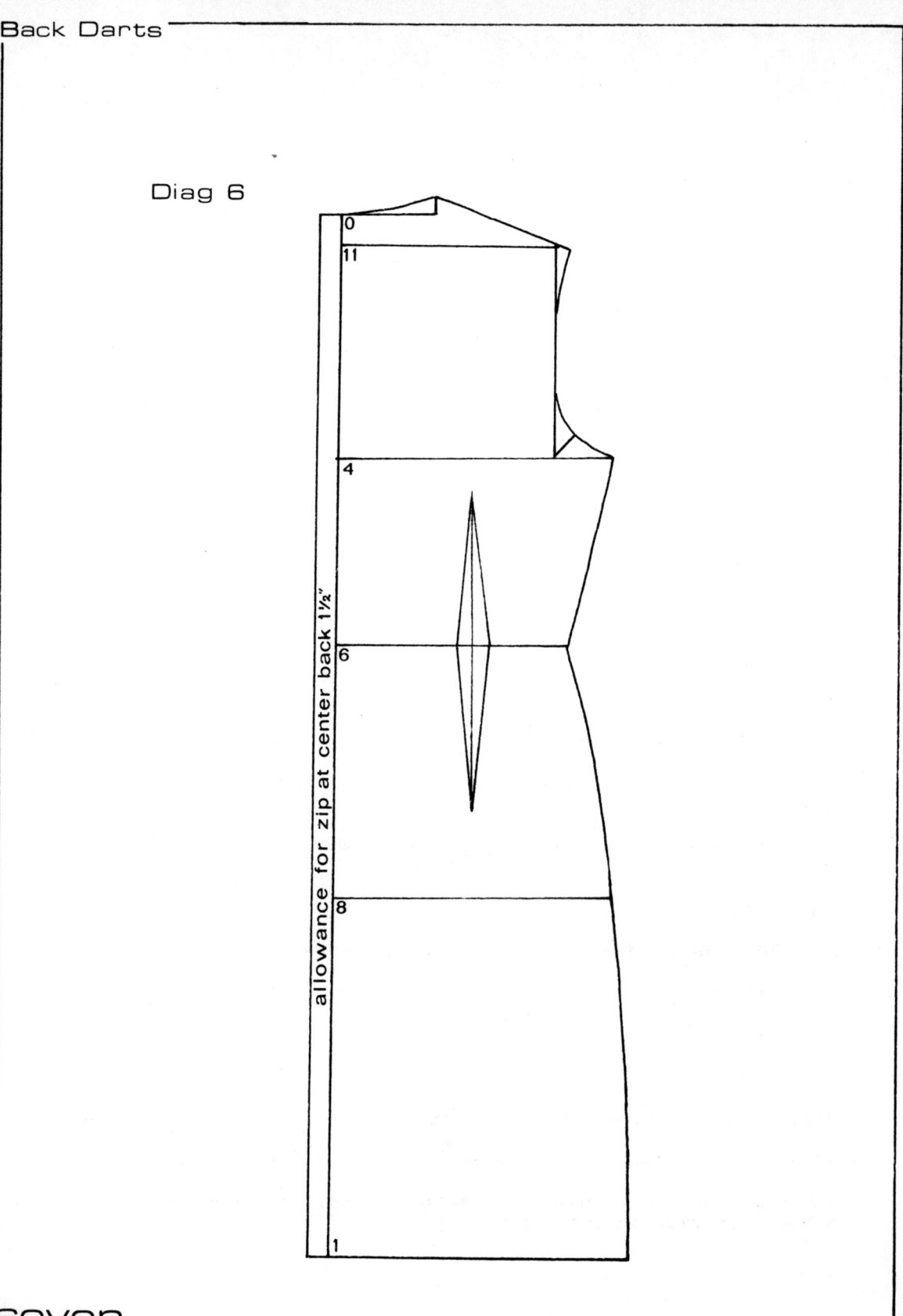

Diag 6

seven

Back Darts

Back darts should **not** be cut through as positioning of them depends on the figure or shape at **seat**. Dress should first be tacked or basted together and fitted on, then pin up **excess** amount of material at **waist** to nothing at most prominent part of seat and upwards to below shoulder blades. By using this method you will find correct position and suppression required.

Once this is done, mark the position of darts on to your back block pattern, for all future dresses.

Skirt Back Block

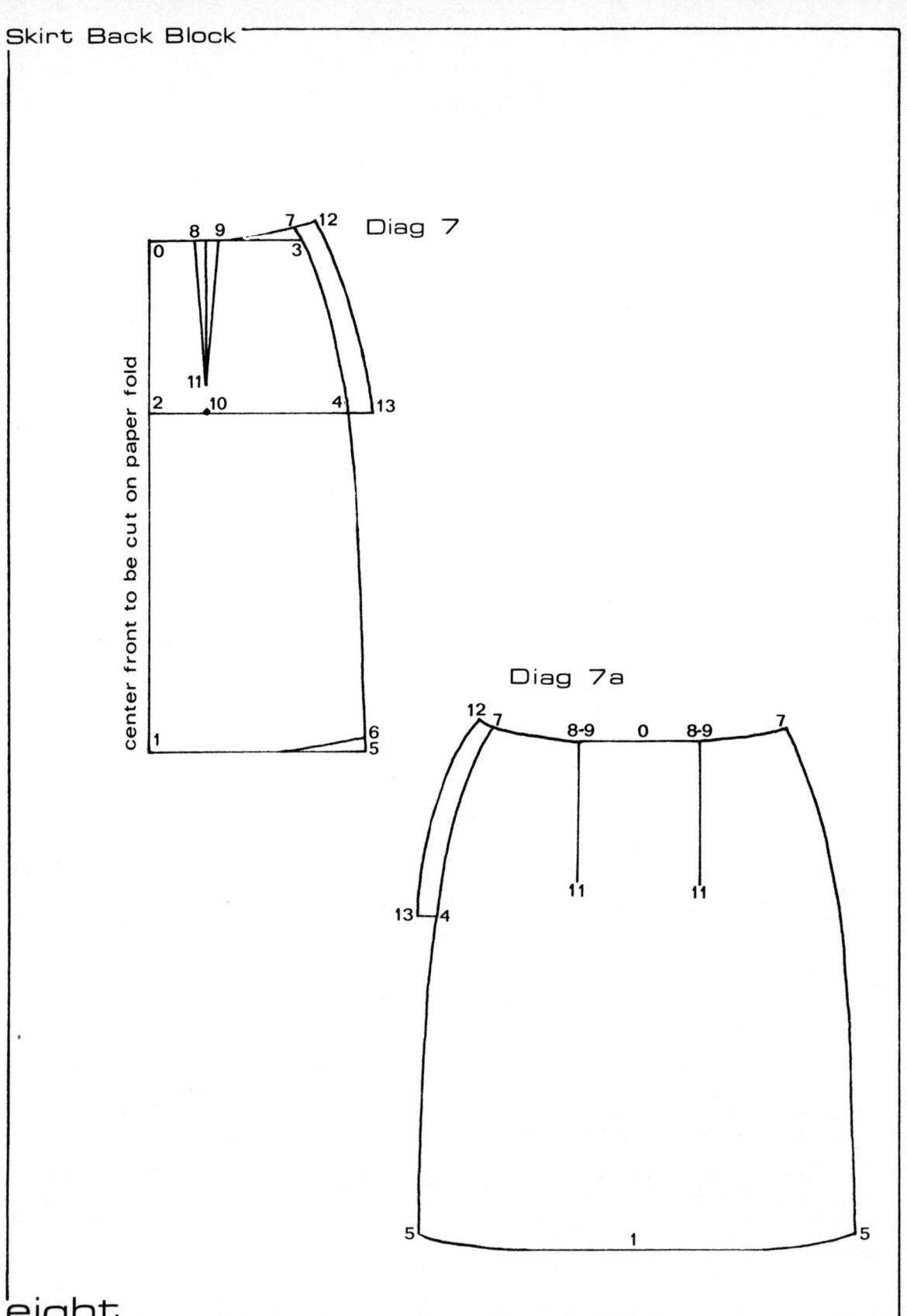

Diag 7

Diag 7a

eight

Skirt Back Block

This block pattern is used for any style of skirt by simple adaptations as can be seen on the following pages.

Diag 7

0 to 1 is length of skirt plus ½" which is cut on fold of paper.

2 is 7½" from 0 for hip line.

3 from 0 is ¼ waist measurement plus 1" for seams and back darts.

4 from 2 is ¼ hip measurement plus ½" for seams.

5 is squared out from 1 to required width of bottom of skirt.

Run line from 3 shaping to 4 and straight down to 5.

6 is ½" up from 5.

7 is ½" up from 3.

Shape waist line from 7 to 0.

Shape bottom from 6 to 1.

8 is 3" from 0.

9 is 1" from 8.

10 is 3½" from 2.

11 is 1" up from 10.

Run line from 8 and 9 down to 11. This is for back darts.

12 and 13 are both 1½" allowance for sewing in zip.

Your **Front Skirt** is cut by using your back pattern as they are both cut identically. The only difference being that no front darts need to be made unless this is for a person with a prominent stomach. Should this be necessary add extra allowance at waist side seam from 3 running down to nothing at 4 (hip line).

You will always find that when a skirt has no front darts it fits cleaner and gives a more slender line as it avoids excess fulness over the stomach.

Skirts with Knife Pleats, Inverted or Box Pleats

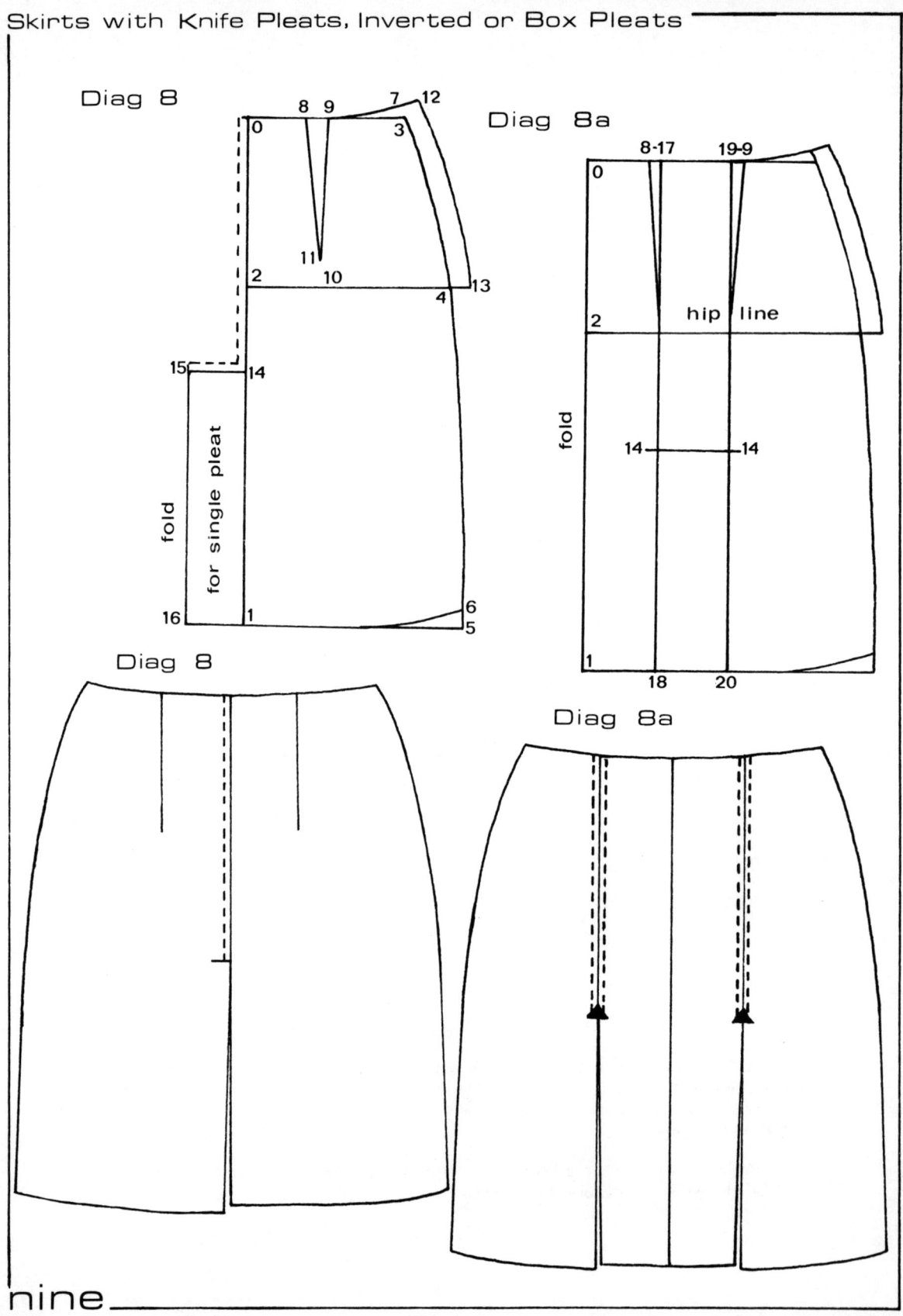

nine

Skirts with Knife Pleats, Inverted or Box Pleats

Firstly we deal with the **Knife Pleat** skirt, for this a double sheet of paper is required.

Start your pattern 2½" away from front edge of paper, marking this out the same as your skirt block pattern in diagram 7.

You then add your allowance for pleat by the following instructions.

Diag. 8.

14 from 1 is length of pleat required (diagram shows 10" pleat).

14 to 15 is 2½".

1 to 16 is 2½".

Run line from 1 to 16 and 14 to 15.

This section is folded over to give a centre back, single Knife Pleat.
As diagram 8. Broken lines are machine stitches.

For **Inverted Pleat** skirt, section 15 and 16 should be 5" not 2½" otherwise it is cut exactly the same way as for Knife Pleat. When making skirt, pleat is pressed inverted.

Broken line in diagram 8 is ½" allowance for seam, this is your cutting line.

Diag. 8a

To cut a skirt with a **Double Knife Pleat** or **Box Pleat**, centre front 0 to 1 should be cut on fold of paper. You do **not** add your allowance at 15 and 16 but extend 5" at side seam, from 7-4-6 this is for two pleats of 2½" each.

17 and 18 are both 3½" from centre front at 0 and 1.

19 and 20 are both 5" from 17 and 18.

8 and 9 are both ½" from 17 and 19 for the back darts, running to 1" above hip line.

14 is your length of pleat.

8 and 14 are sewn to 9 and 14.

14 down to 18 and 20 is your pleat. This can either be pressed over to form a Box Pleat or pressed inverted. More pleats can be added as required, each time adding the extra width of material per pleat.

Flaired Two Piece Skirt

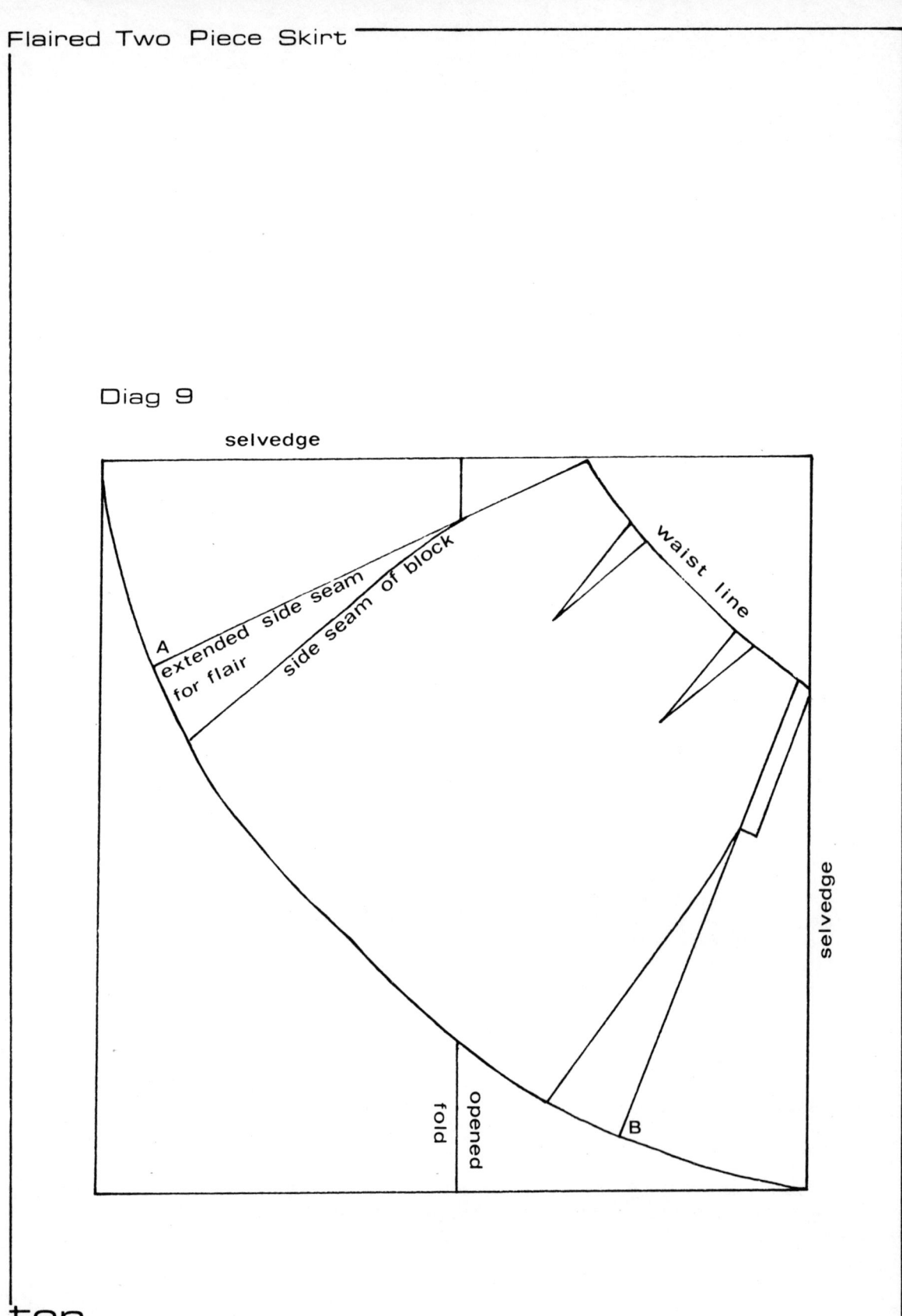

Diag 9

Flaired Two Piece Skirt

This is a Flaired Two Piece Skirt cut on the bias of your material. To give it a very full flair you can use the whole width of your material.

Two lengths of material are required for this skirt of approximately 1 yard each. Open them both out and lay one on the other, then place block pattern diagram 7 diagonally on your material as diagram 9 shows.

A and B are side seams extended from block pattern, this can be extended from selvedge to selvedge of material. You will then have a very full flaired skirt.

Roll and Standing Collars

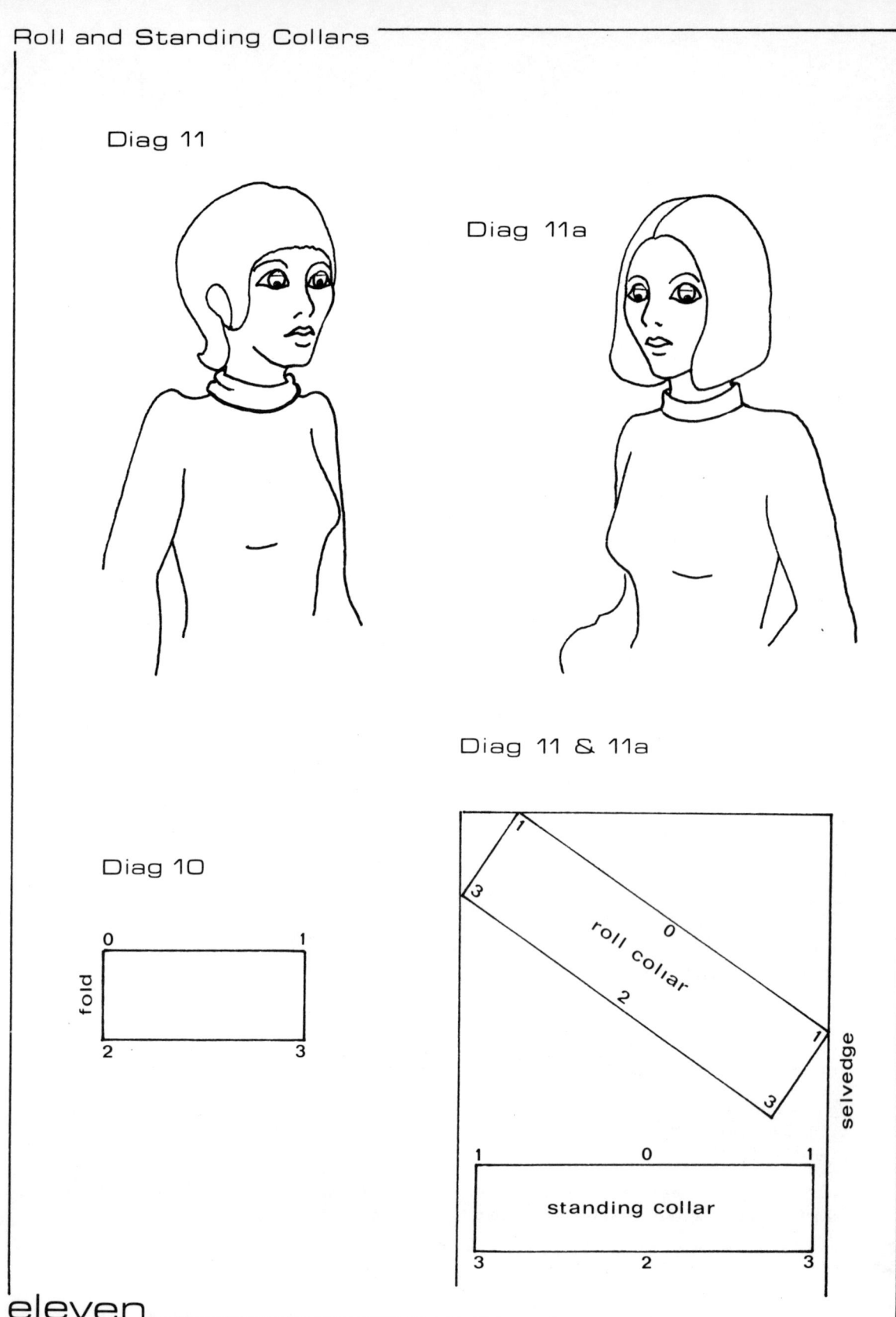

Diag 11

Diag 11a

Diag 11 & 11a

Diag 10

eleven

Roll and Standing Collars

For Roll or Standing Collars both patterns are cut the same, the difference is in the **cutting of the material**.

To cut your pattern as diagram 10 you require a double sheet of paper.

Diag 10

0 is on fold.

0 to 1 is distance around front and back neck of dress pattern. Refer to diagrams 1 and 2 on page for this measurement which is from 0-3-16.

0 to 2 on diagram 10 is double required width of collar plus ¾" for seams. Average width for this collar is 3¾". For Roll Collar cut pattern 1" wider.

3 is squared out from 1 and 2.

Cut your pattern and open it out, this will give you full length of collar in one piece.

Diag 11

Shows lay for Roll Collar which is cut diagonally on the material.

Diag 11a

Shows lay of pattern for Standing Collar, this is cut horizontally with grain of material.

Collar material should be folded from 1 to 3 for sewing on to garment.

Shirt Collar

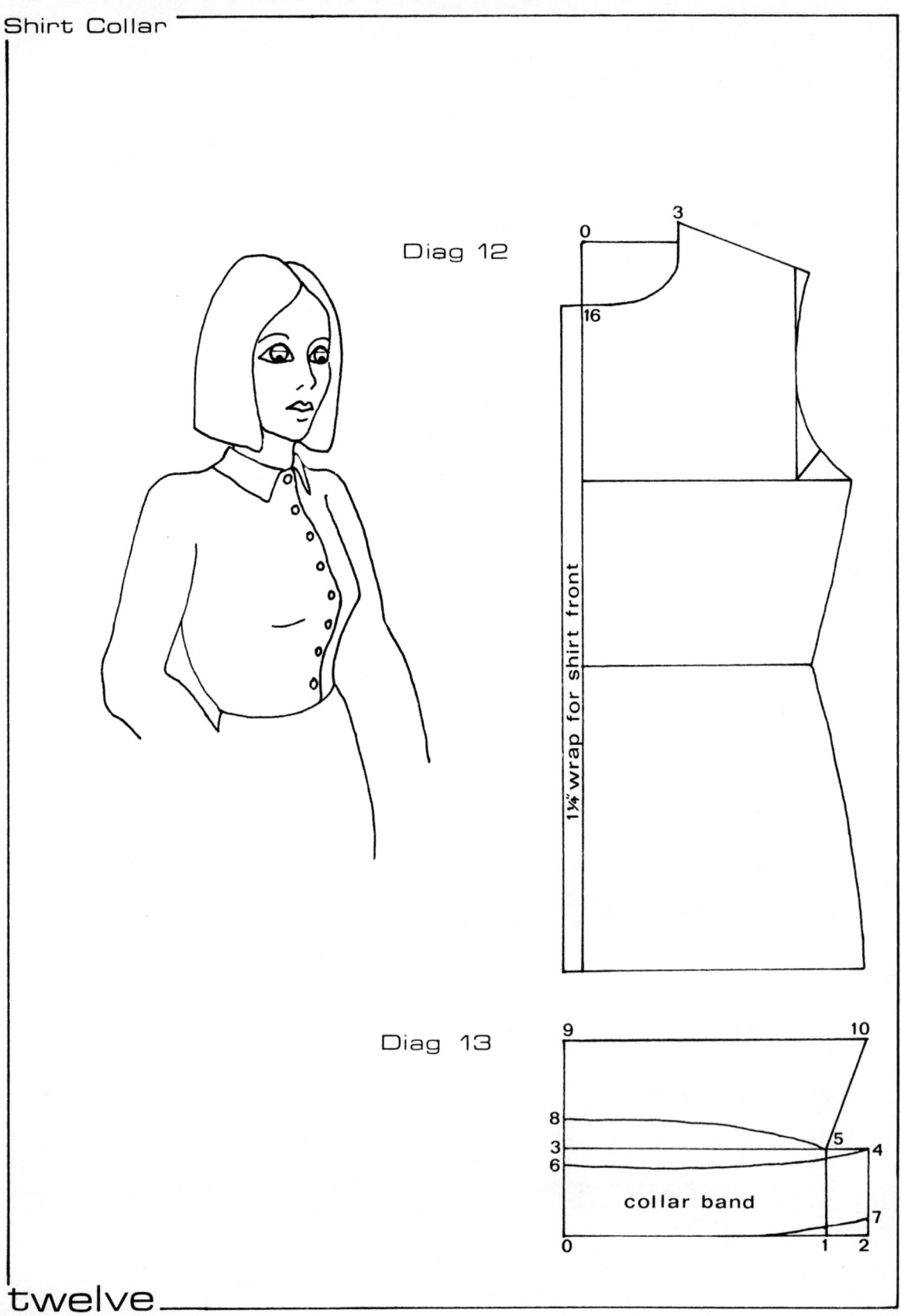

Diag 12

Diag 13

twelve

Shirt Collar

The ever popular Shirt Collar never seems to date. The neckline can be worn open or closed, as in sports shirts or shirt-waister type dresses. Garments made with shirt collars should have cut through fronts with 1¼" wrap as diagram 12 shows.

The following instructions are for cutting Shirt Collar:

Diag 12

Neckline of dress 0 to 16 is 2". Run shaped line from 3 to 16 on to front edge of wrap.

Diag 13

0 to 1 is neck measurement from centre front of dress at 16 to 3 and on to 0 of back dress pattern.

1 to 2 is 1¼".

3 is 2½" from 0.

4 is squared from 2 and 3.

5 is squared from 1.

6 is ½" from 3.

Shape line from 4 to 6.

7 is ½" from 2.

6 to 8 is 2". Shape along to 5.

8 to 9 is 2¾".

10 is squared up from 4 = 3¾". Run line from 9-10-5.

This completes your pattern for a Shirt Collar.

Section 6 and 8 are sewn together along to 5. Top collar should be cut the same way plus ¼" longer and wider.

Peter Pan Collar

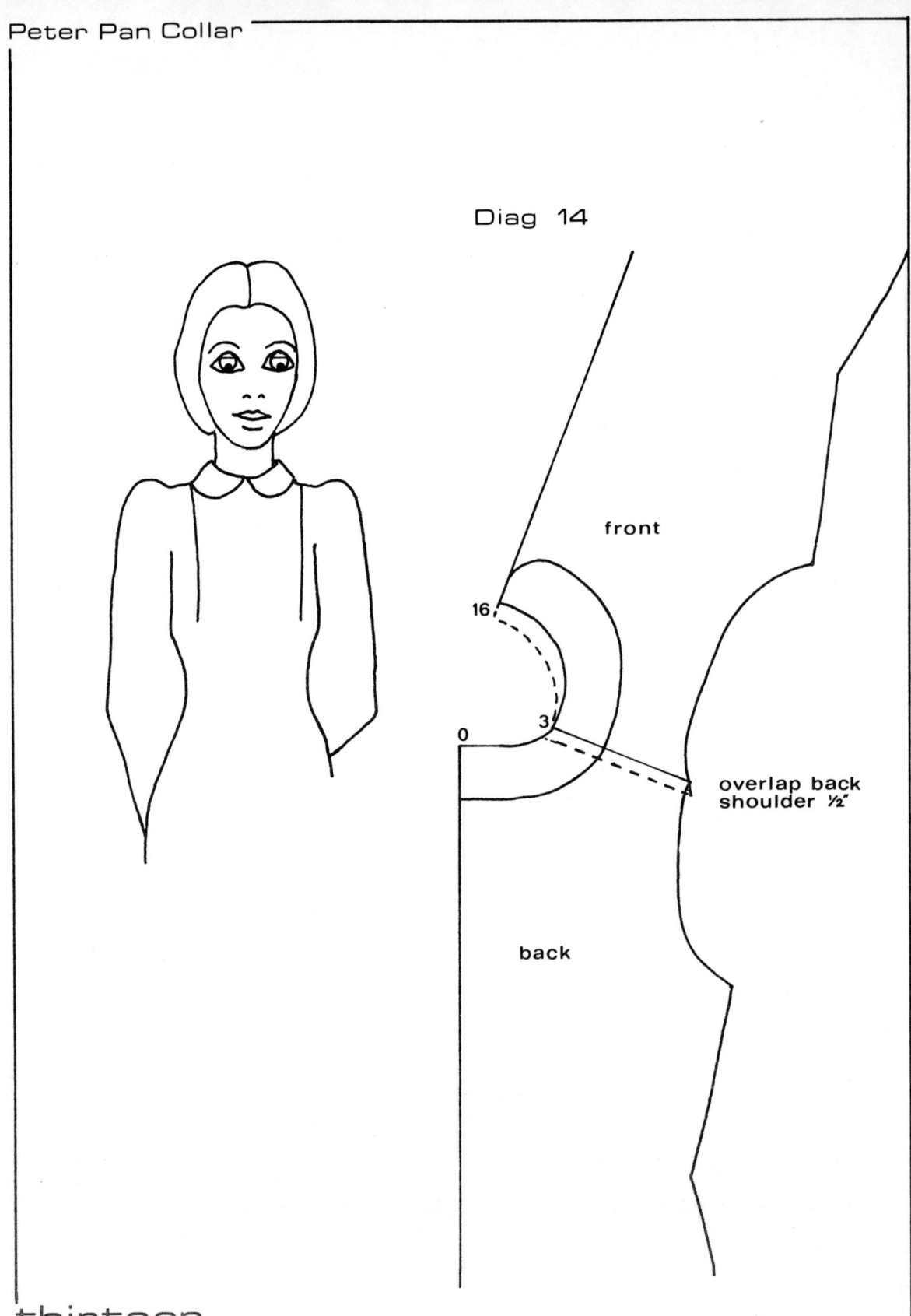

Diag 14

thirteen

Peter Pan Collar

The Peter Pan Collar can be made of the same material as your dress, but this is only recommended when the dress is made of a plain unpatterned material.

Here then are your instructions:

Front and back patterns should be pinned together at shoulders **overlapping** ½" as diagram 14 shows.

You then mark round your neckline 16-3-0.

Broken line point 16 can be ½" to give a closer neck fitting. Once you have your neckline, remove your dress pattern and mark your collar to any required width.

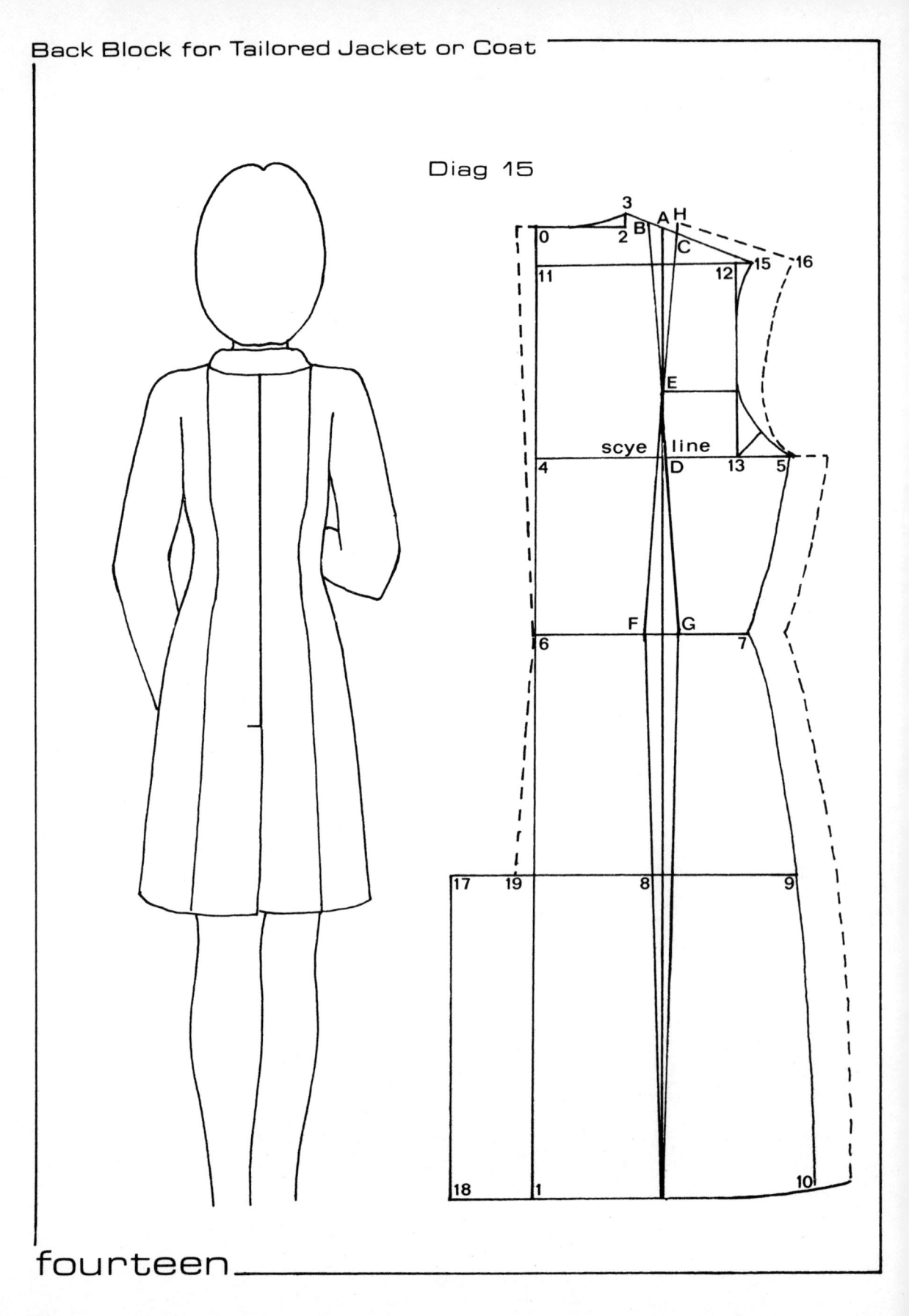

Back Block for Tailored Jacket or Coat

Diag 15

fourteen

Back Block for Tailored Jacket or Coat

When taking measurements for jacket or coat you must add 2'' on bust, waist, and hip measurements and 1'' on cross back.

Single layer of paper is required for this.

Drawing your pattern as you would for a dress with the increased measurements. Start your centre back 3'' away from edge of paper.

A cut through back from shoulder seam down to bottom, will give a well shaped garment as diagram 15 shows.

Instructions for cutting:

Diag 15

A is 2'' from 3. Run straight line from A to bottom of coat.

B and C are both ½'' from A.

E is 2'' up from D (scye line).

F and G are both ½'' hollowed out at waist line.

Run line from B-E-F and down to bottom of coat, then run line from C-E-G to bottom of coat.

Now add material at side seams, shoulder and armhole to allow for the cut through back.

H from E is same distance as B from E.

16 from 15 is 2''.

Armhole parallel at E is extended 1½''.

Side seams are extended 1½''. Broken line at shoulder, armhole and side seams are your new cutting lines.

The cut through from shoulder to bottom can be moved nearer to side seams or to centre back. For a stout person it is advisable to shift it nearer to the side seams to go over most prominent part of seat.

To add a centre vent the back must be cut through with the following allowances:

Extend ½'' at 0 to nothing at waist and ½'' at 19 as broken line shows.

17 and 18 are both 3'' squared out from 19 and 1.

This now completes your jacket and coat pattern.

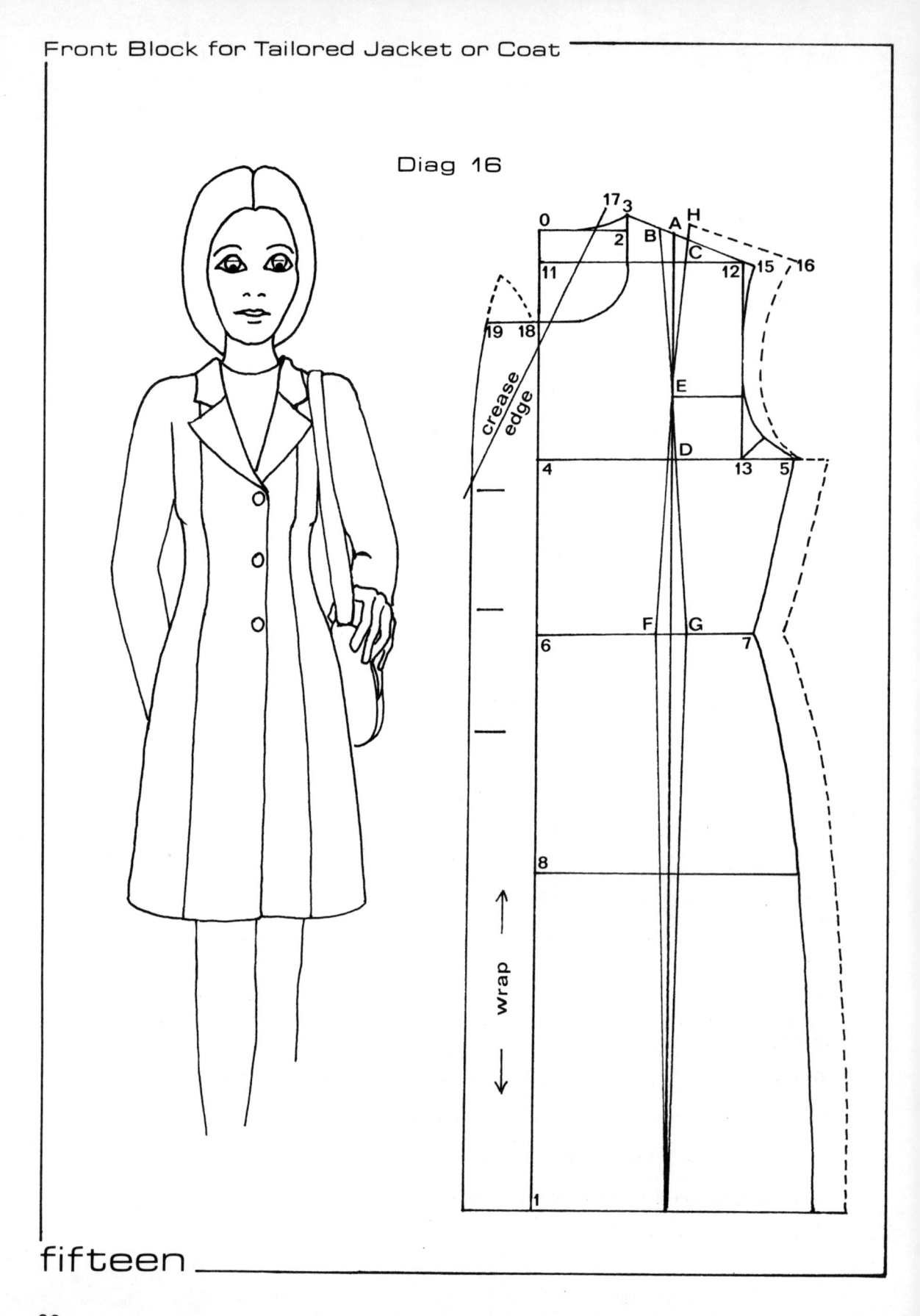

Front Block for Tailored Jacket or Coat

Diag 16

fifteen

Front Block for Tailored Jacket or Coat

This is drawn the same way as your back block pattern. Should you require a cut through front the same as back, follow the same instructions as for coat back.

You can use your back coat pattern for this minus the vent, making adjustments to neck and adding allowance on front for wrap as follows:

Diag 16

The centre back of your pattern 0 to 1 is now the centre front of coat or jacket.

Add 1½" on fronts 0 to 1 for **jacket** wrap. For **coat** this should be 2½" as shown by arrow.

17 is 1¼" out from 3. Run line for crease edge from 17 to where you choose to make your top button hole.

18 is 3½" from 0. Shape neck from 0 to 18 on to any width required at 19.

Shape lapel from 19 down to top buttonhole. Wrap at fronts can be made wider should you want a **Double Breasted Coat**, say 4".

Broken line at 18 and 19 shows shaping for Double Breasted lapels.

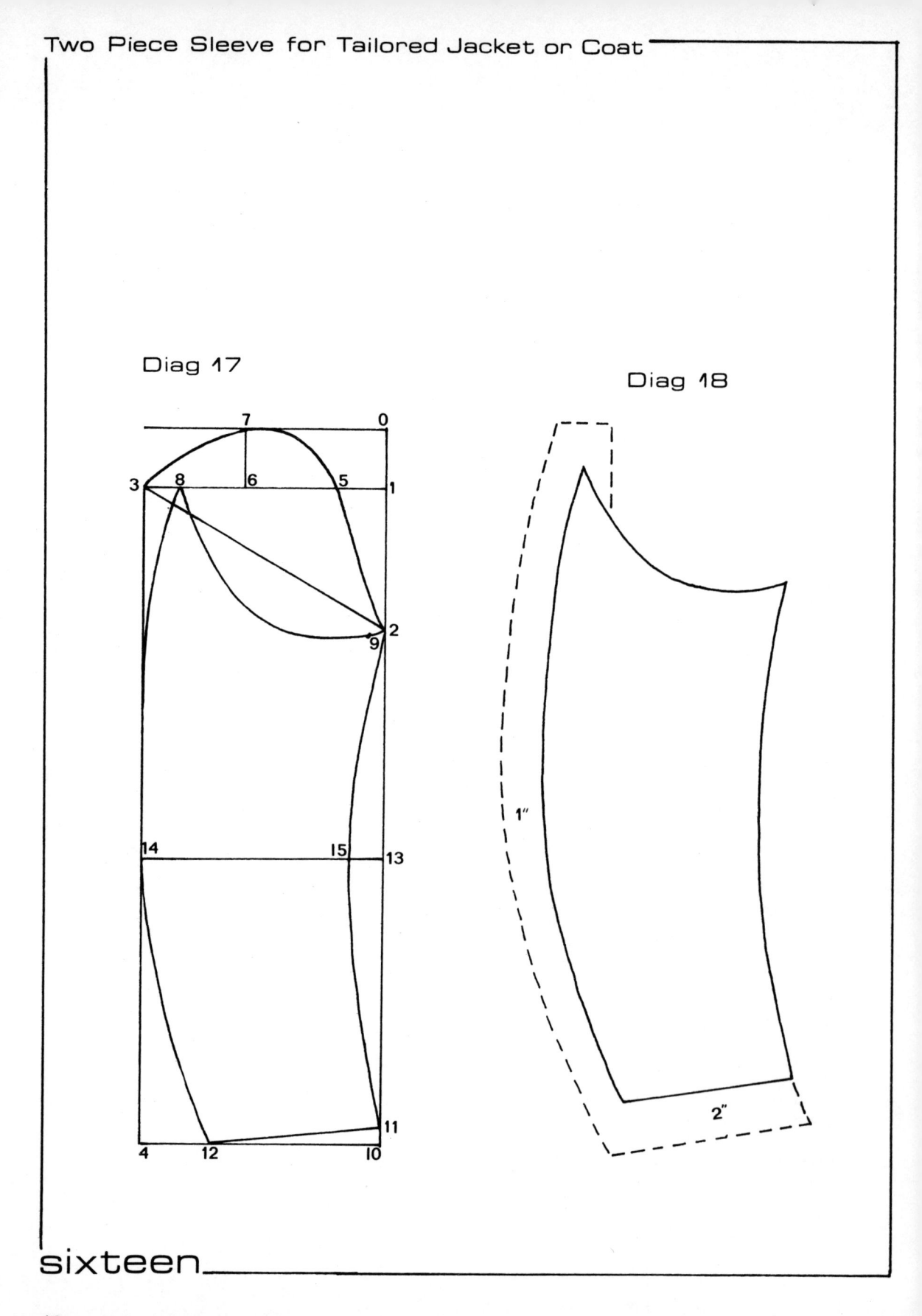

Two Piece Sleeve for Tailored Jacket or Coat

Diag 17

Diag 18

1"

2"

sixteen

Two Piece Sleeve for Tailored Jacket or Coat

The Two Piece Sleeve is recommended for a tailored or fitted coat or jacket as this will give a slim, slender line.

Diag 17

This shows how the top and under sleeves are marked out together.

0 to 1 is 2".

0 to 2 is same distance as 0 to 4 of your back block pattern minus 2".

2 to 3 diagonally is the same distance as back armhole of block pattern at 5 going round to 14 and on to 15.

4 is squared down from 3 to full length of sleeve plus $\frac{3}{8}"$.

5 is 2" from 1.

6 is half way between 3 and 5.

7 is squared up 2" from 6.

Shape top sleeve head from 3 to 7 around 5 and down to 2 coming in slightly at 2.

8 is 1" from 3.

9 is 1" from 2. Run straight line from 2 to 9 and shape to 8 as indicated for under sleeve.

10 is squared out from 4.

11 is 1" up from 10.

12 from 11 is required width of cuff say 5½".

13 is half way between 2 and 11.

14 is squared out from 13 for elbow.

15 is 1" from 13.

Shape front seam from 2 to 15 and down to 11.

Shape hindarm seam from 8 to 14 and down to 12.

This completes the marking out of your top and under sleeve. Now cut around your top sleeve only at numbers 2-15-11-12-14 and on to 3-7-5 and 2.

Place pattern on to another sheet of pattern paper and cut another top sleeve. Then cut your under sleeve around numbers 2-9-8 and down to 14. You now have your top and under sleeve complete. When cutting your material you should always leave inlays as diagram 18 shows. 1" at broken lines and 2" on length of top and under sleeves.

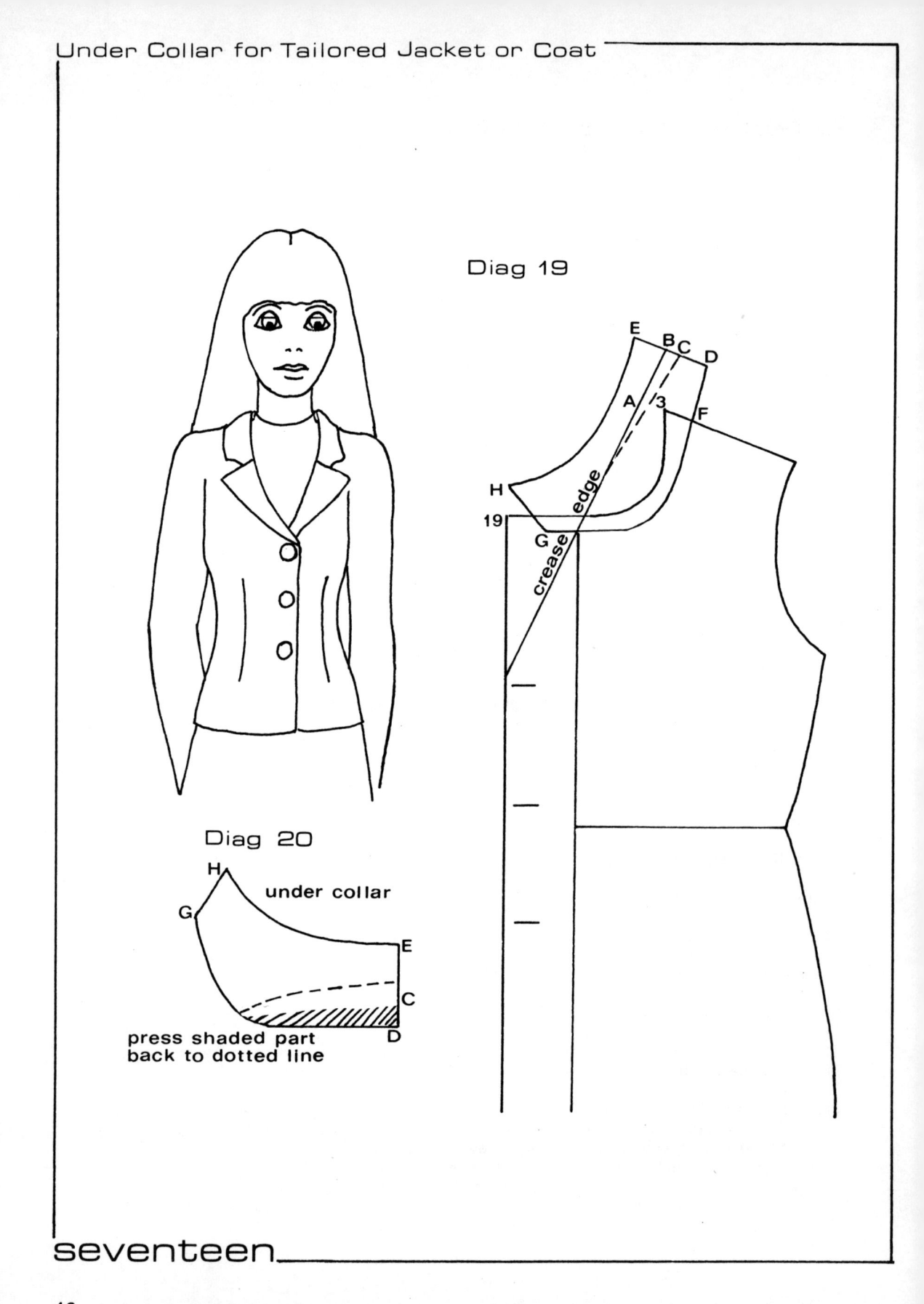

Under Collar for Tailored Jacket or Coat

Diag 19

Diag 20

under collar

press shaded part
back to dotted line

seventeen

Under Collar for Tailored Jacket or Coat

This is for either a double or single breasted jacket or coat, with **fall back collar** and **lapels.** The crease edge is pressed flat from point C to about 2" down lapel. This will give a soft roll to the garment.

Diag 19

A is 1¼" squared out from 3.

B from A is distance of back neck pattern from 0 to 3.

C is ½" from B. Broken line is crease edge.

D is 1½" from C.

E is 2" from C. Run line from E to D. This is centre seam of collar.

F is 1¼" from 3.

Run line from D through F to ½" inside neckline as indicated.

G is approximately 1¼" from edge of lapel at 19.

H is required width of collar. Run shaped line from H to E coming in slightly at A.

Material for this collar must be cut on the bias.

Before basting collar to neck of coat, collar must be stretched by using press iron. Wet the material slightly and stretch between F and D then between E and H. Press crease edge from C along crease edge line, now shrink material along crease edge so that collar will have a rounded shape. Diagram 20 shows under collar. Shaded section is the stand of collar. This has to be pressed back to broken line. Your top collar should be cut horizontally ¼" longer and wider than under collar and stretched in the same way.

Garments Requiring Facings

Front Facings

For a jacket or coat, front facings should always be cut to allow for slight easing when sewing on to your garment. The collar and lapels of your garment should always have the facing sewn on with slight ease, both in length and width, this will allow them to fall correctly and avoid curling. These facings should be cut ¼" longer and wider to go over the crease edge of lapel so that when garment is made up lapels are covered by the facings.

Facings for Necks, Armholes or Pockets

Easing is not required for these therefore they should be cut net to shape and size. The width can be left to your own choice.

Front Block for Trousers

Diag 21

eighteen

Front Block for Trousers

This block can be adjusted to any required style: Slimline, 'Oxford Bags', or Flaired Bottoms.

Half seat measurement is your trouser scale.

Diag 21

0 to 1 is ¼ waist measurement.

0 to 2 is difference between outside and inside leg measurement.

2 to 3 is ¼ seat measurement.

Shape line down from 1 to 3.

2 to 4 is ⅙ scale minus ½".

2 to 5 is ⅙ scale plus ½".

6 is $\frac{7}{8}$" from 2.

Shape through 4-6-5.

3 to 7 is half way between 3 and 4 plus ½".

7 to 8 is inside leg measurement plus ½".

9 and 10 from 8 are both ¼ of required width of bottoms.

11 is ½" up from 8.

Shape line through 9-11-10.

For zip sides add 1½" at 1 down to 3.

Back Block for Trousers

Diag 22

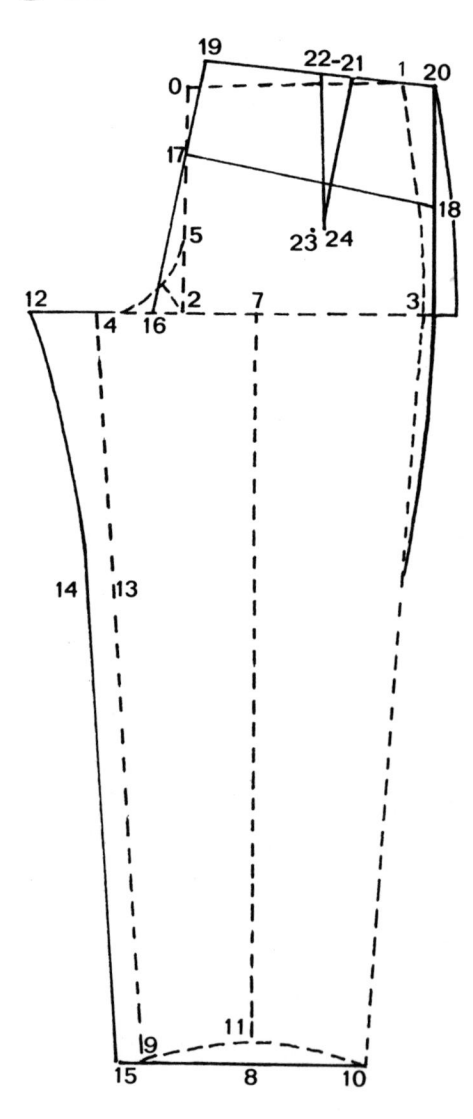

Back Block for Trousers

Diag 22

Dotted line indicates trouser front which should be marked out on your pattern paper.

12 is 2½" from 4.

13 is half inside leg length less 2" from 4.

14 is 1" from 13.

15 is 1" from 9.

16 is half way between 4 and 2.

17 is $\frac{1}{3}$ of scale from 16.

18 is squared out from 17, ¼ seat measurement plus ½".

Run line down from 18 coming out at dotted line to 3, same distance from dotted line as 18. Then run line down to 10 coming in to dotted line at knee which is level with 13.

19 is continued up from 17 extended 1" from dotted line.

Shape seat line as indicated from 12 to 17.

20 from 19 is ¼ of waist measurement plus 1½", running through 1.

Shape from 20 to 18.

21 is 3" from 20.

22 is 1" from 21.

23 is squared down from 22 being 6½" long.

24 is ½" from 23.

Run lines down from 21-22-24, these are your back darts.

All seams are allowed for.

Allow 1½" at 20 down to 3 for zip facing.

For Flaired Bottoms, width can be extended at 10 and 15 to nothing at knee, this is done on both sections of trouser bottoms.

For 'Oxford Bags' width can be extended at 10 and 15 to hip line at 12 and 13. For turn-up bottoms **do not** shape bottoms at 11 but allow approximately 4" on length to turn-up.

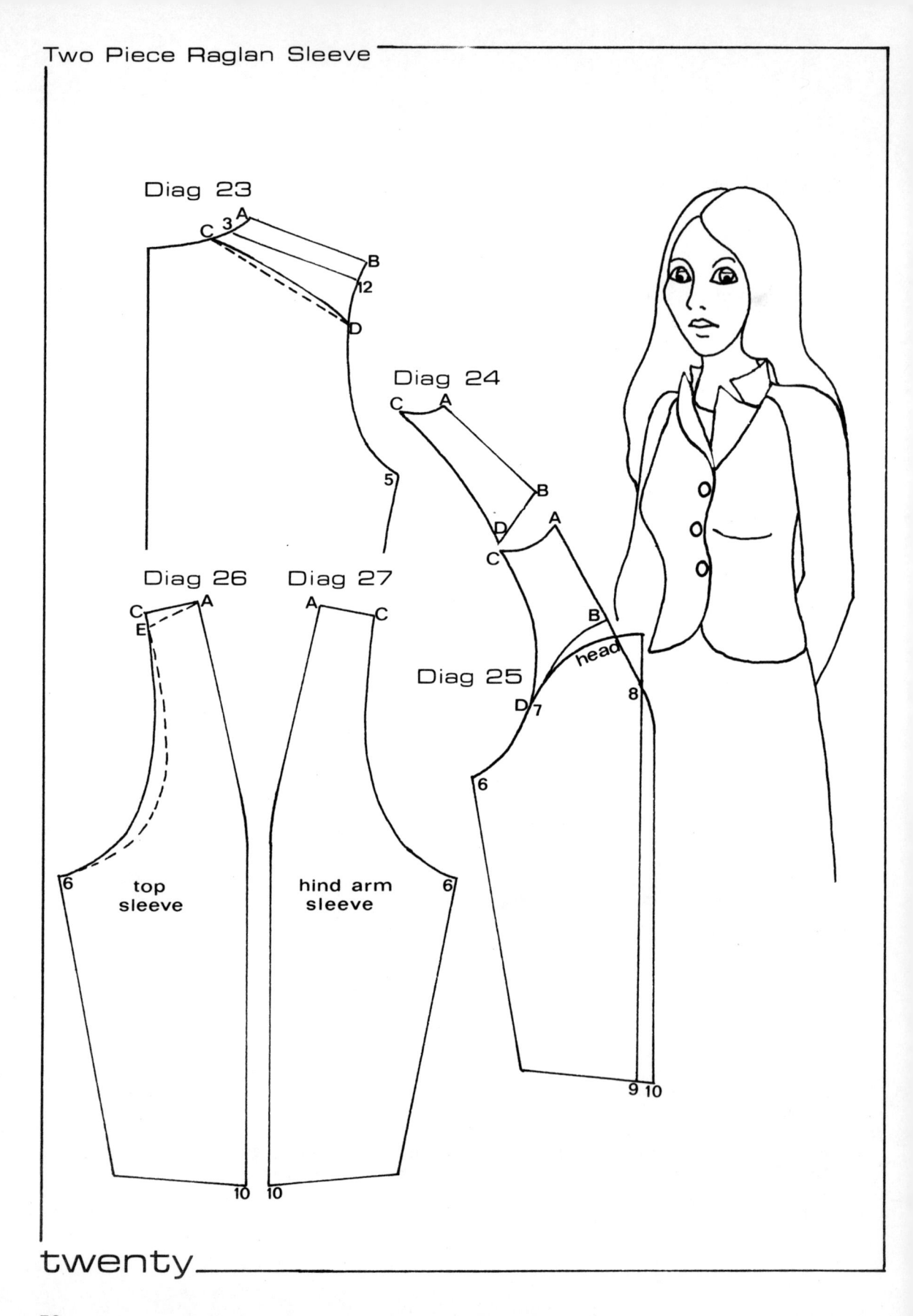

Two Piece Raglan Sleeve

Diag 23

Diag 24

Diag 25

Diag 26 — top sleeve

Diag 27 — hind arm sleeve

twenty

Two Piece Raglan Sleeve

The purpose of a Raglan Sleeve is to give ease and comfort but most important it must be cut to give a neat and tidy line without showing any excess material as this will cause discomfort and can look very ugly.

By careful following of these instructions you will have a perfectly fitting sleeve.

Draw your back block pattern as diagram 1 in the usual way, marking numbers 3-12 on shoulder line and 5 at side seam.

Diag 23

A and B are both 1" from 3 and 12.

C is 1½" from 3.

D is 2½" from 12. Run broken line from C to D then curve slightly as shown, this is your cutting line. Cut off this section through D to C and around A to B down to D. Diagram 24 shows this section.

Now mark out a normal One Piece Sleeve about 1" from folded edge of paper.

Diag 25

Now measure the same distance on your sleeve from 6 to 7, as 5 to D on diagram 23.

Take section diagram 24 which you have already cut from your back pattern and place this to your sleeve head point D, touching at 7.

B should be $\frac{3}{8}$" up from sleeve head.

Mark this out as diagram 25 shows, rounding at D and 8 which is approximately 3" down from sleeve head.

10 is 1" from 9 which is your sleeve width.

Run curved line from 8 down to 10. Cut this out along lines 6-D-C-A-B-8-10 and along to 6. You now have two sections of sleeve. Recut either of them for your top sleeve.

Diag 26

Shows top sleeve. C to E is 1". Draw **broken line** from E to A.

Broken line from 6 to E is hollowed out ¾".

Recut sleeve from 6-E-A. This completes both top and under sleeves as both diagrams 26 and 27 show.

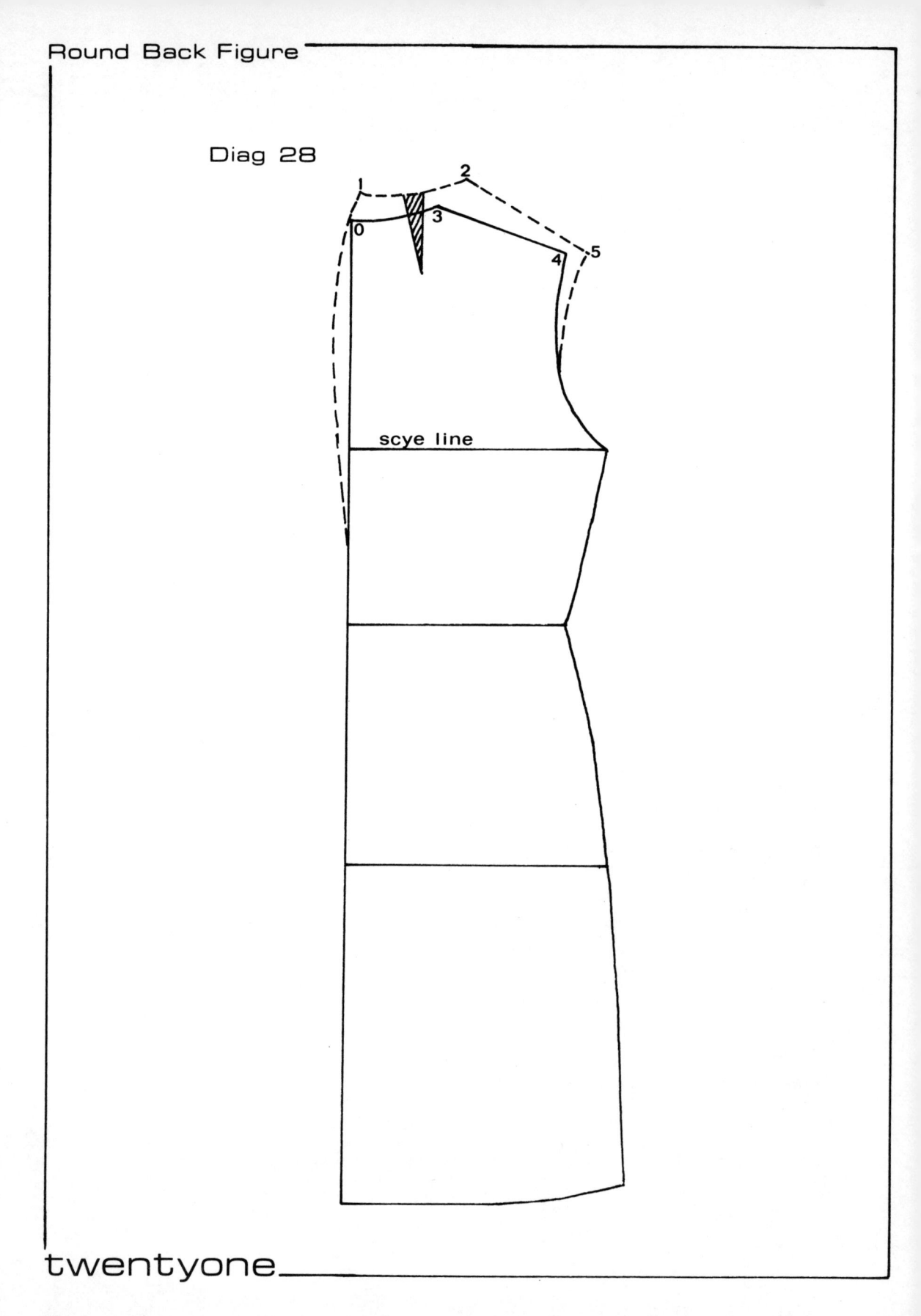

Round Back Figure

Diag 28

scye line

twentyone

Round Back Figure

When cutting a garment for a round or hump backed figure the following adjustments are required:

Mark out your back in the normal way as diagram 1 but **not** on fold of paper, starting 1" from edge.

Diag 28

Broken line at centre back and shoulder shows adjustments according to the shape of the figure. For this a centre back seam is required, allowing 1" seam for zip.

1 is 1" up from 0 and $\frac{3}{8}$" forward which is continuation of round of back. This is done to give extra length on back to compensate distance from scye line, otherwise dress will stand off at back of neck.

1 to 2 is same distance as 0 to 3 and 1" up.

4 is your normal shoulder width.

5 is $\frac{3}{8}$" from 4.

Shaded part at back neck is dart 1" wide to nothing at bottom, this is half way between 2 and 3.

This should give a perfect fit to back neck of garment.

When cutting material it is advisable to leave 1" extra inlay at centre back, as it is quite possible when fitting garment you may find that more round is required than has been allowed. With the extra material you can make the adjustments required.

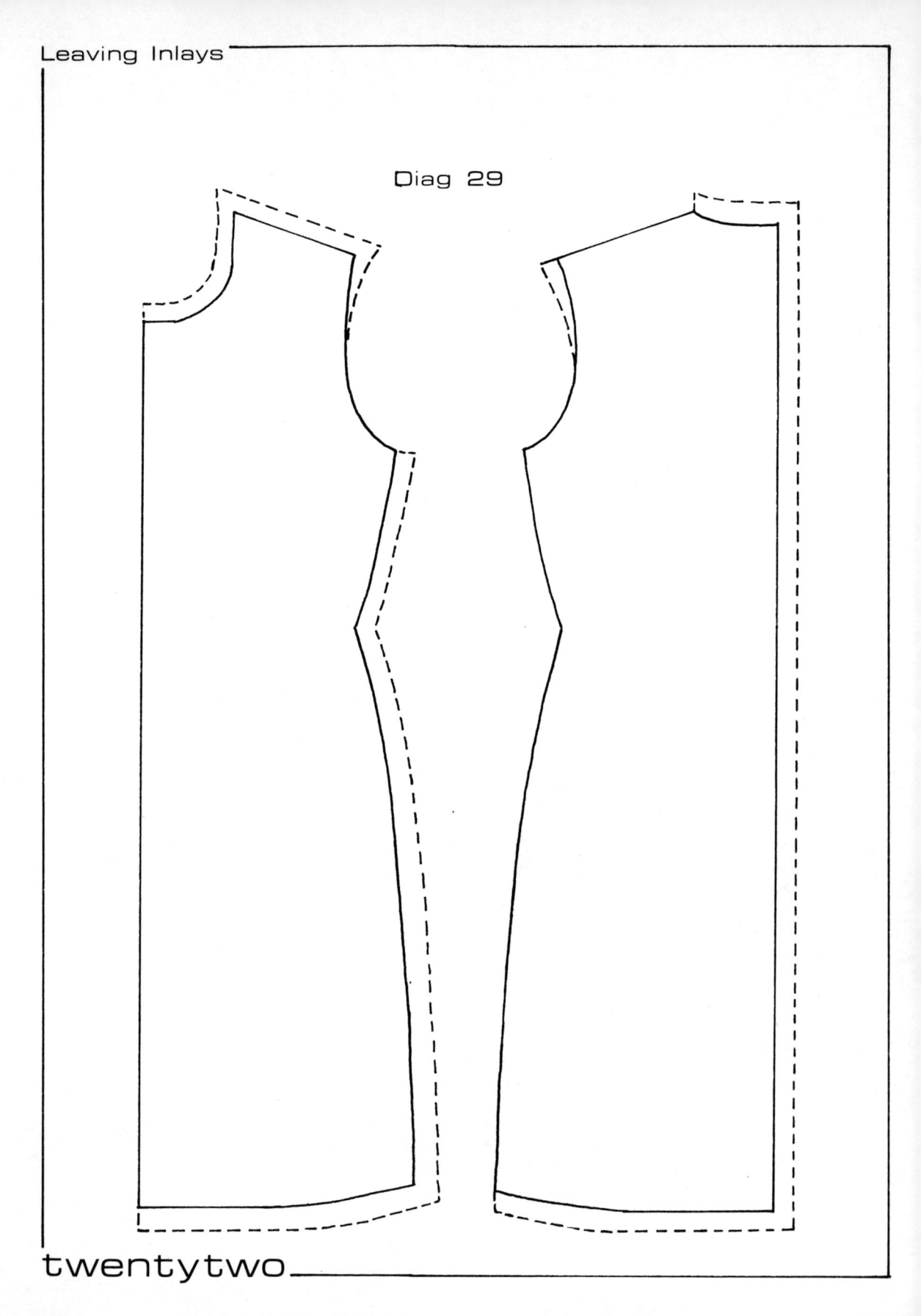

Leaving Inlays

Diag 29

twentytwo

Leaving Inlays

It is always advisable to leave inlays, otherwise known as turns, when cutting garments. This is a very good precaution as often after taking measurements people may change their foundation garments and measurements are completely different.

The most suitable places to allow for your inlays are your front shoulders, armholes at top, front side seams and at neck front and back, as broken lines show on diagram 29.

You may also leave turns at centre back.

Dress Design A

twentythree

Dress Design A

This design will be used on the following pages as an example of how you can cut and lay out your own designs from your block.

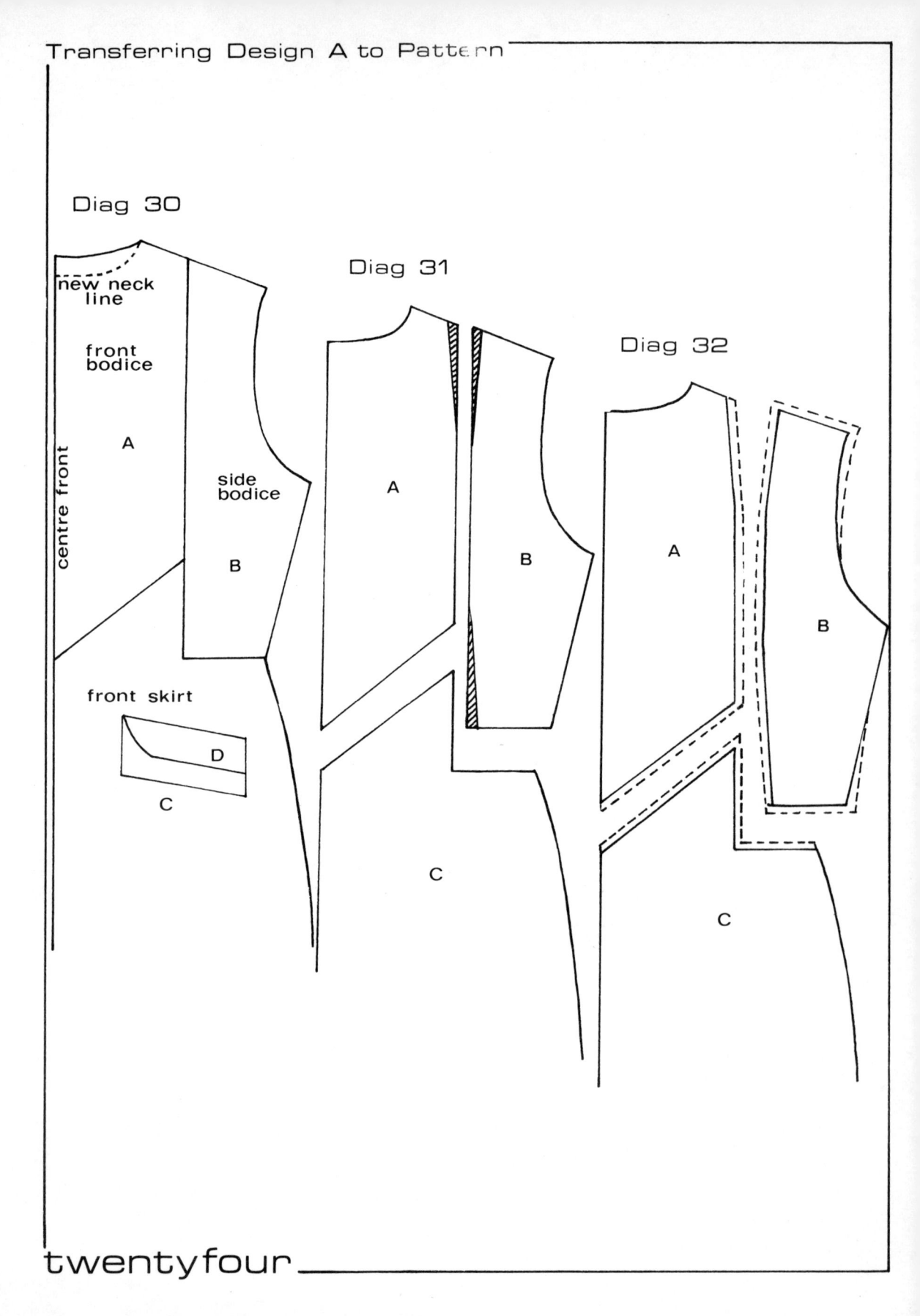

Transferring Design A to Pattern

Diag 30

new neck line

front bodice

centre front

A

side bodice

B

front skirt

C D

Diag 31

A

B

C

Diag 32

A

B

C

twentyfour

Transferring Design A to Pattern

The first step is to trace a copy of your basic block pattern.

Your basic block pattern should now be kept as your Master Block for cutting future garments.

With your sketch in front of you draw your design onto the traced copy of your Master Block. These sections are then cut out and placed onto another sheet of pattern paper and marked out with seam allowances around all sections of your design (not at side seams, shoulder or armholes as these have been allowed for on your Master Block).

We use Dress Design A as an example:

Diagram 30 is the front of dress marked out on the traced copy of your Master Block.

Diagram 31 shows front bodice, side bodice and skirt (sections A B C) after having been cut out. Shaded sections are for shoulder and waist darts which are sewn through the seams.

Diagram 32 shows sections A B C placed on another sheet of cutting paper, broken lines indicating ½" seam allowances which are your new cutting lines. Broken lines on section B at armholes and side seams are allowances for shoulder and waist darts.

On the following page you have instructions for cutting the collar, pockets, sleeves, cuffs and back.

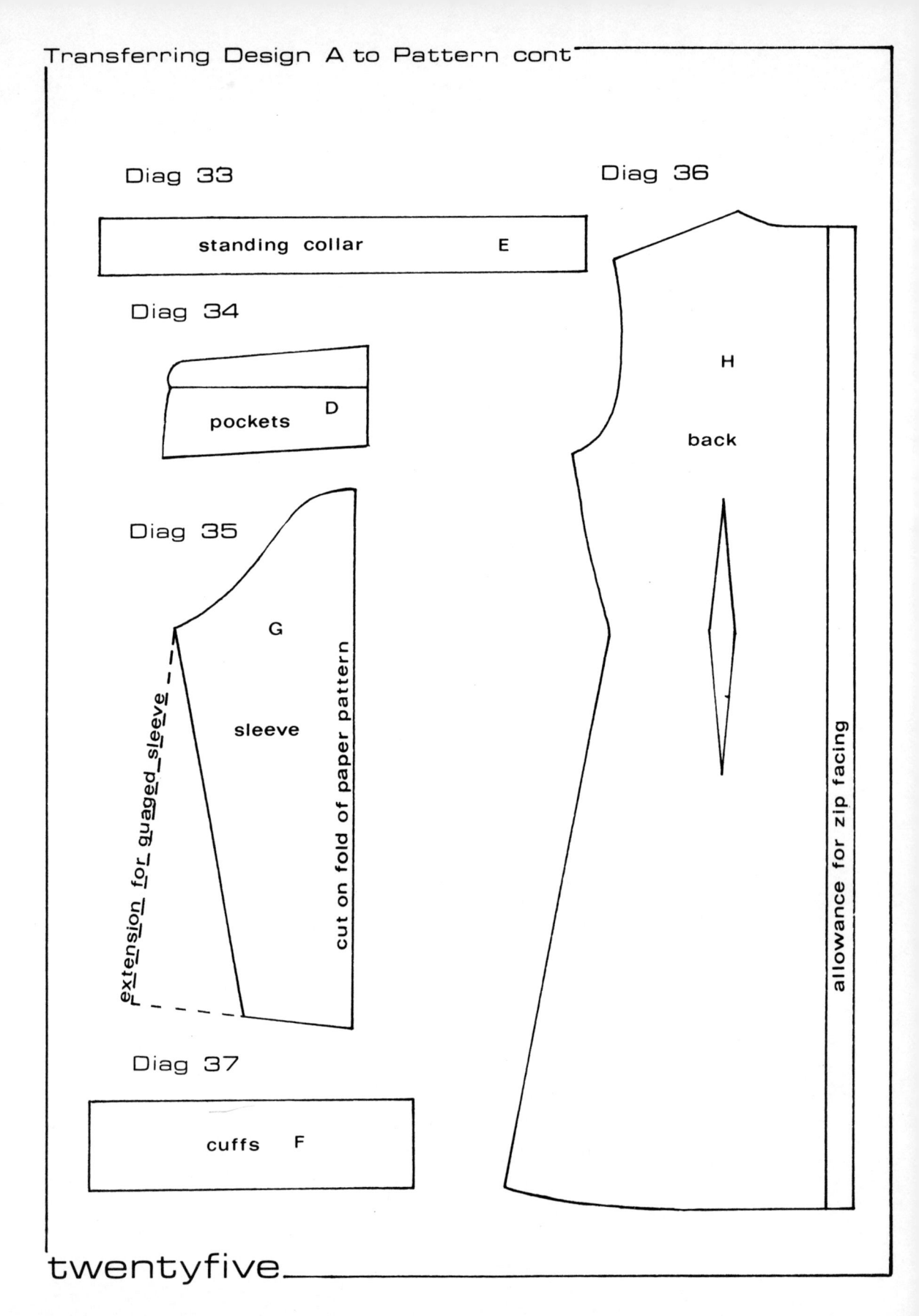

Transferring Design A to Pattern cont

Diag 33

standing collar   E

Diag 34

pockets   D

Diag 35

G

sleeve

extension for guaged sleeve

cut on fold of paper pattern

Diag 36

H

back

allowance for zip facing

Diag 37

cuffs   F

twentyfive

Transferring Design A to Pattern cont

These are your instructions for cutting out the collar E, pockets D, sleeves G, cuffs F and back H for Dress Design A.

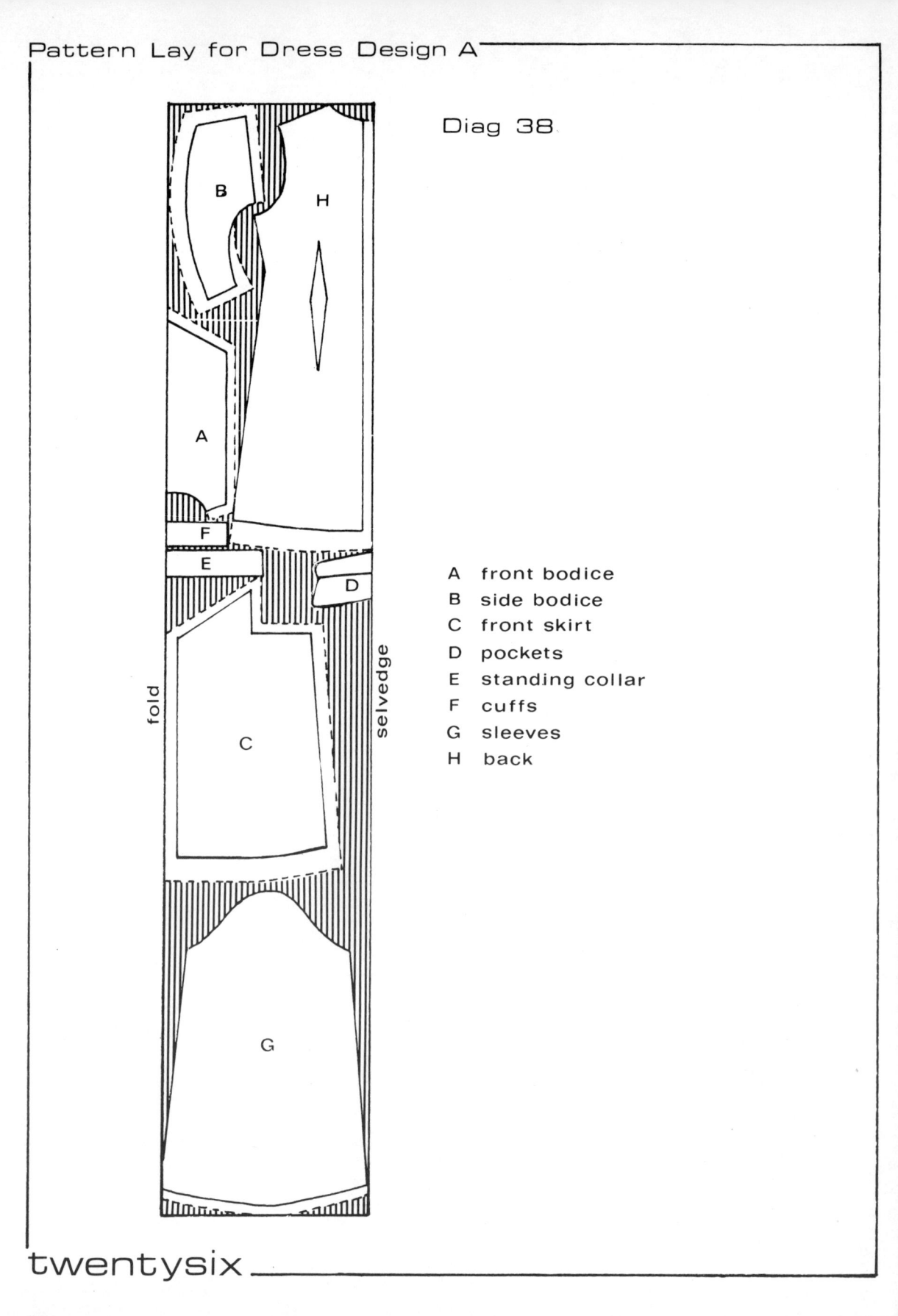

Pattern Lay for Dress Design A

Diag 38.

fold

selvedge

A front bodice
B side bodice
C front skirt
D pockets
E standing collar
F cuffs
G sleeves
H back

twentysix

Pattern Lay for Dress Design A

Diagram 38 shows the lay of patterns on your material, broken lines indicating 1" inlays at side seams of bodice and front skirt.

To avoid buying more material than is necessary the following should be very helpful:

Lay your patterns out on the table or floor. Assuming the material is 18" wide when folded, lay your patterns to fit into the 18" width and continue lengthwise. Once all your patterns are laid out, measure the length used and this will give you your required yardage.

Blazer Styles Single and Double Breasted

twentyseven

Blazer Styles Single and Double Breasted

On the following page you have full instructions on the cutting of both Single and Double Breasted Blazers.

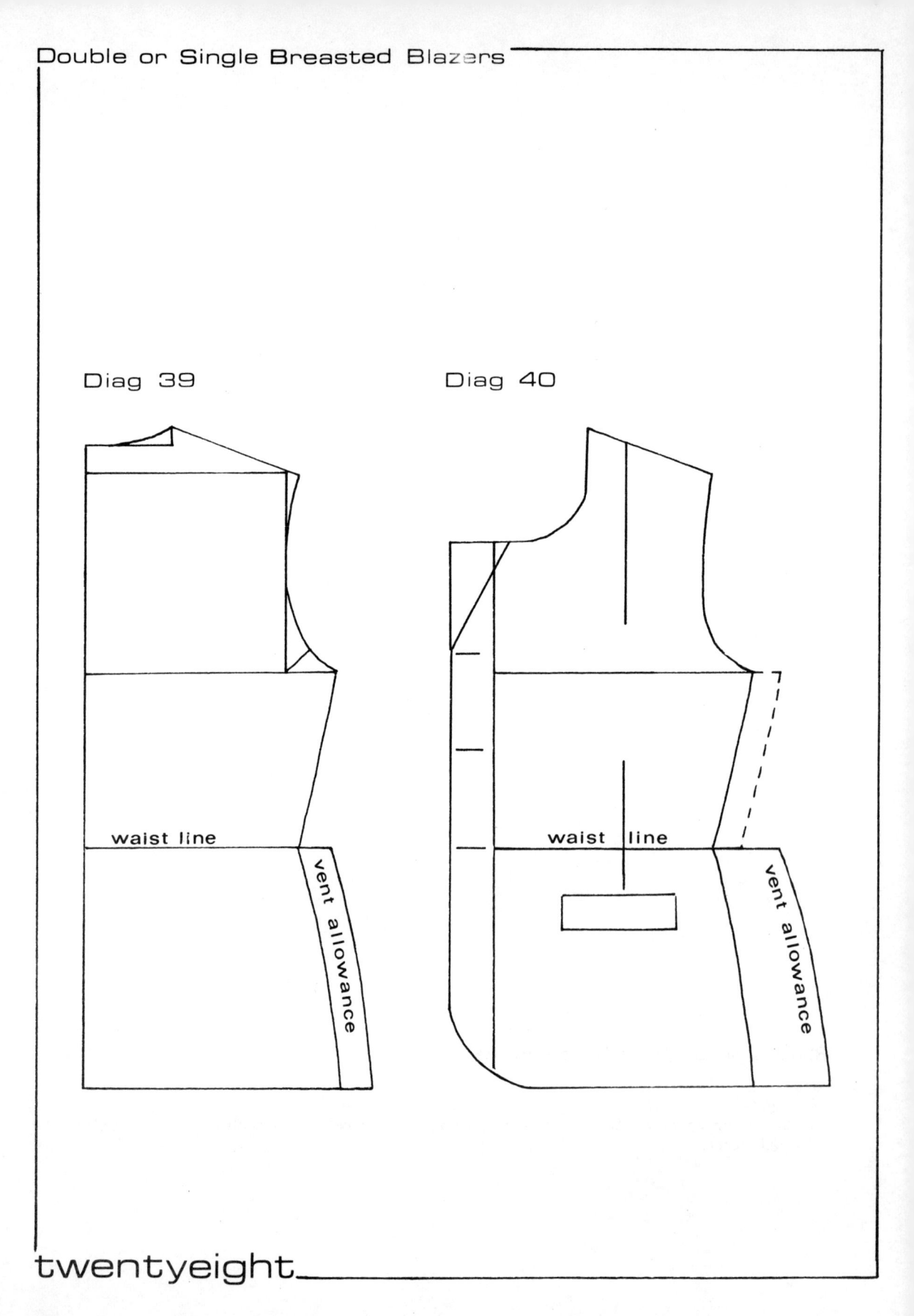

Double or Single Breasted Blazers

Diag 39

Diag 40

waist line

vent allowance

waist line

vent allowance

twentyeight

Double or Single Breasted Blazers

To cut a Double or Single Breasted Blazer follow the same instructions as for coat or jacket patterns. For Double Breasted allow 3" for the front wrap, for Single Breasted allow 1½" wrap. If you do not wish to make a cut through front and back, but only shoulder and waist darts, this can be done by using the same instructions as for dress diagrams 5 and 6 on pages 20-23.

Blazer with centre back vent

This is done in the same way as coat vent, see instructions on page 37.

Blazer with side vents

Allow 3" extra inlay on **front side seam** from waist down to bottom of garment and 1" inlay on side seam of back as shown on diagrams 39 and 40.

For Single Breasted round front blazer, you round off the bottom of fronts to your own personal style and shape.

Draping for The Beginner

twentynine

68

Draping for The Beginner

You do not require a pattern for a draped garment as this is best done by pinning and cutting on the figure, or better still on a Dress Form.

The Dress Form is very useful for this purpose as it can be tiring for the person being fitted. This may take a considerable time to get the garment to fit correctly as a lot of repinning is usually required.

The beginner should not indulge in a too expensive material at this stage. Firstly it is difficult to know the correct amount of material you will need, and secondly it requires a lot of skill and experience before one can accomplish the art of draping correctly. It is very helpful when starting to drape your garment to have a diagram or picture of the garment in front of you before starting. In this way you can follow the correct fall and balance of styling.

To create a design on the figure you can lay the end of a length of material over the shoulder, diagonally over the bust to the waist. This can then be cut off and draped to the most suitable style for the figure. Another length is then used over the other shoulder likewise, you then start from the waist downwards. Once you feel pleased with the way these sections have been pinned together, start on the back of your dress.

You will be amazed with the various styles you can create by this method. It is mainly trial and error, or pinning and repinning until you succeed in really feeling pleased with the results. Once you are satisfied with the style and fit, the garment is ready for tacking together, fitting on again, making any necessary adjustments, and then ready for sewing.

Should you wish to take a pattern of the dress, you must mark or number your sections of the garment and enter them on a sheet of paper or into a book. Once you have got the details entered, the pins are taken out of the garment. Lay your material onto your pattern paper, tracing your darts, folds or pleats. Seams should be allowed for where necessary before cutting your pattern. Once this is done, tack your dress together, fit it, and proceed with its completion.

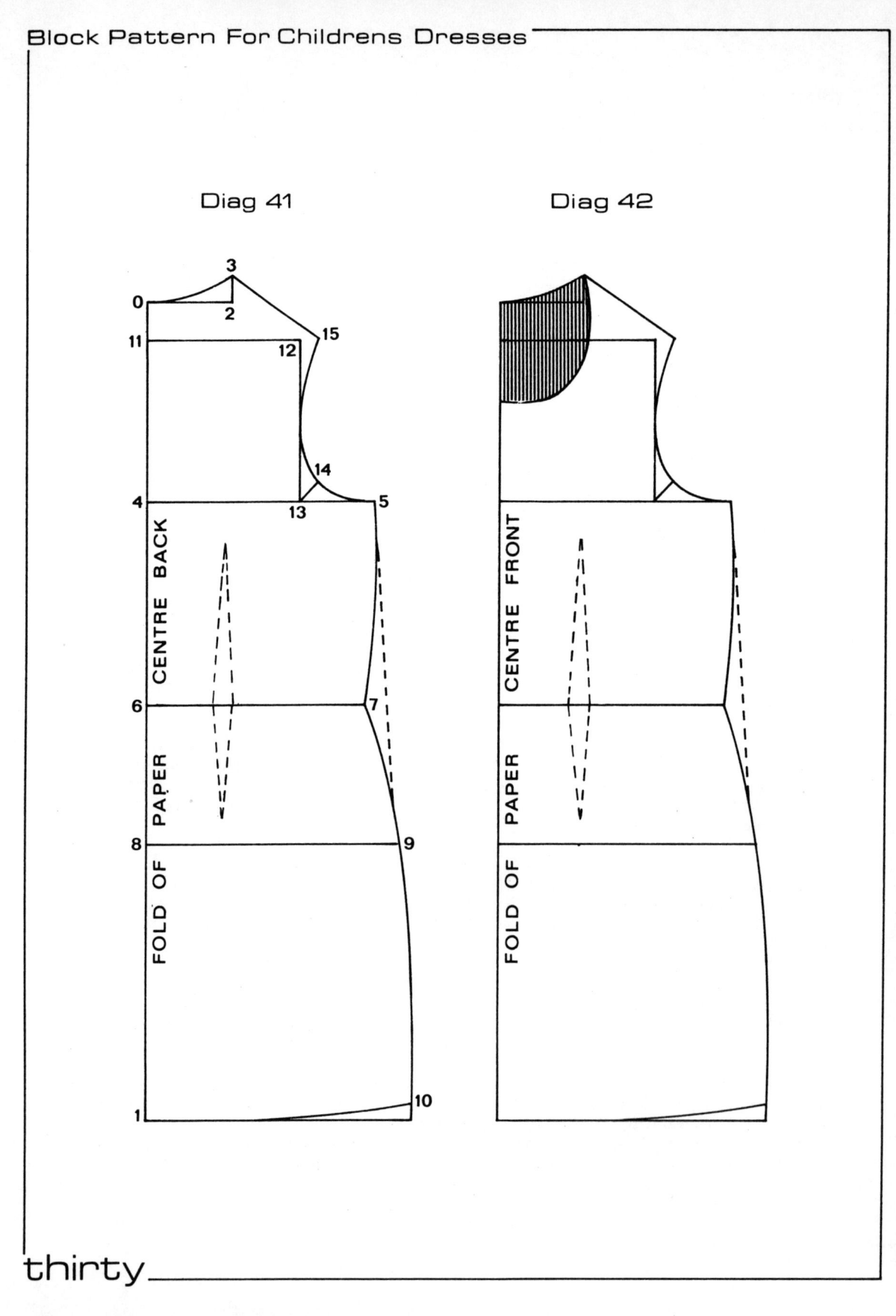

Block Pattern For Childrens Dresses

Diag 41

Diag 42

thirty

Block Pattern for Childrens Dresses

Diag 41 and 42

Measurements should be taken as chart shows on Page 10. Half Bust measurement equals scale. Diag 41 is 26". Bust = Scale 13".

Use double sheet of paper folded at 0 to 1 as Diag 41 shows.

0 to 1 is full length of dress

2 from 0 equals $\frac{1}{6}$ **of scale**

3 from 2 equals ½".

4 from 0 is half scale minus ½" for scye line.

5 from 4 is ¼ bust measurement plus ½".

6 is waist line measured down from 0.

7 from 6 is ¼ waist measure plus ½".

8 is hip line measured down from 0.

9 from 8 is ¼ hip measure plus ½".

Draw side seam line through 5 — 7 — 9 — 10.

10 being ½" from bottom line squared out from 1.

11 is 1" down from 0.

12 is squared out from 11 which is half cross back plus ½".

13 is squared down from 12 on to bust line.

14 is ¾" out from 13.

15 is ½" from 12.

Shape shoulder from 3 to 15 and armhole from 15 to 14 and on to 5 shaping on to line 12 — 13 as diag shows.

Front and back darts may be introduced as dotted lines indicate finishing about 1¼" below bust line and 1¼" above hip line. Dotted line at side seams is allowance for quantity taken in at darts.

Cut through fold of paper 0 to 1.

Under layer is your back pattern.

Use the top pattern for your fronts and shape neck to required style as shaded part shows on diag 42.

Sleeves and collars are cut by following instructions as on pages 16, 17, 30, 31, 32 to 35.

Always measure around armhole of pattern to get correct size of sleeve, and neck 0 to 3 of back and 3 to front edge of pattern for size of collar. This completes your block pattern for Childs dress.

Cutting a Dress to Your Own Design

thirtyone

Cutting a Dress to Your Own Design

Mark out your block pattern to required size as diag 41 and 42 shows — using double sheet of pattern paper, and draw your design on to the block. When you have your design completely drawn on to your pattern, it is ready for cutting out.

When cutting your material you allow $\frac{3}{8}$" on each of your design lines, as seams have only been allowed on your block at shoulders, armholes and side seams.

When cutting flaired garments, lay pattern diagonally on material.

See following pages for cutting dresses A and B

Dress A

Diag 43

Diag 44

thirtytwo

Dress A

To help you I have designed and will show you how to cut dresses A and B. Starting with Dress A, mark out your block pattern and draw your design lines as diag 43 shows using double sheet of paper. Broken lines indicate suppression at waist and shoulders to give shape at bust and waist. Broken lines **outside pattern** are for allowance of suppression of shoulder and waist.

Cut out pattern around your design lines.

Use under pattern for your back and top for fronts.

Shape front neck from 3 to 4 coming down from 0 to 4 about 2½" to 3".

Sleeves and collars are cut as instructions on pages 13, 17, 30, 31 and 32 to 35.

Diag 44 shows your back pattern with broken lines indicating where $\frac{3}{8}$" allowance should be made when cutting your material, and 3" wider at bottom of panels to give extra width at bottom, more can be allowed for extra width.

When marking out your material be sure to put front edge of your pattern 4 to 1 on fold of material so that when this is opened out you do not have a seam in centre front of dress.

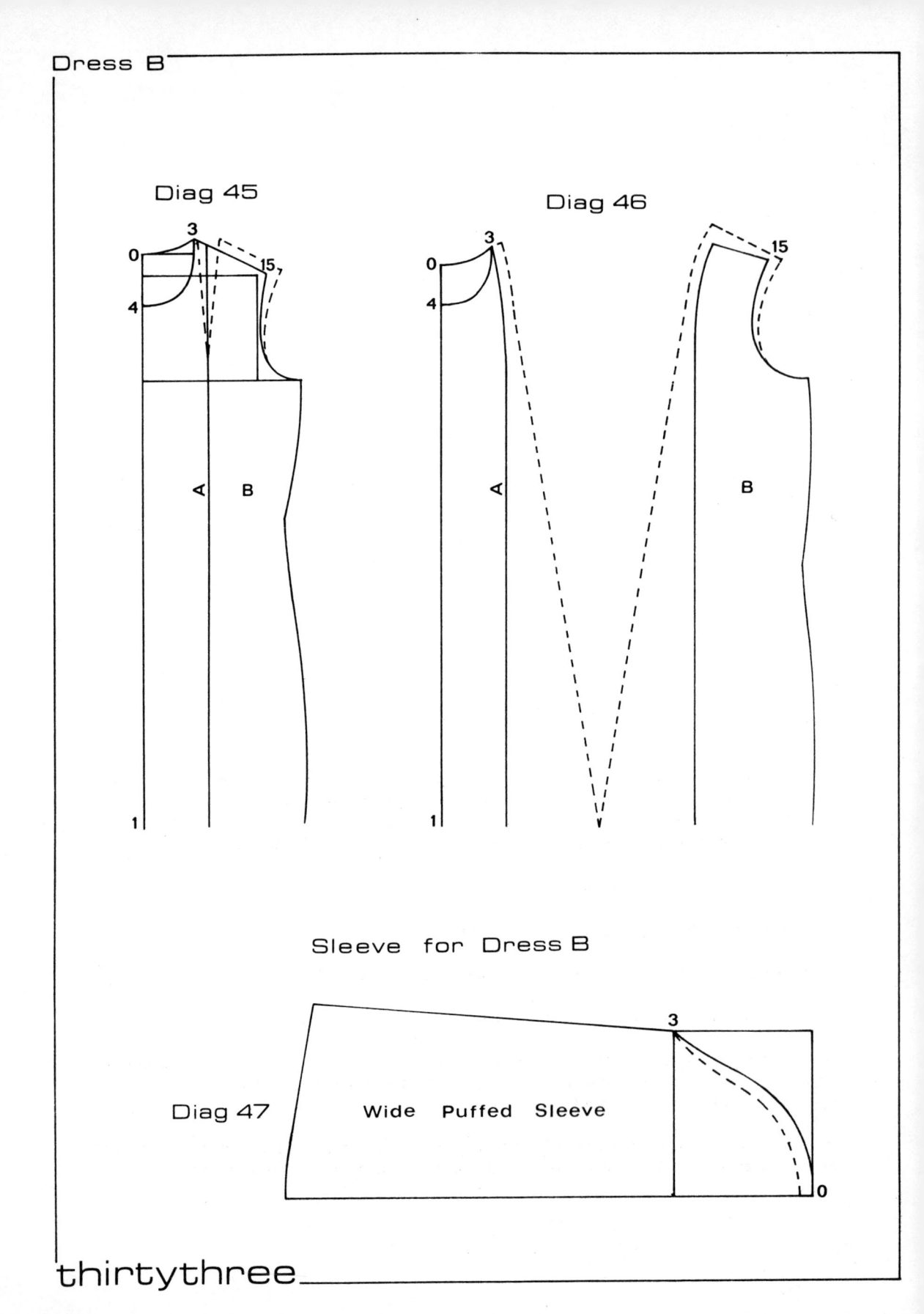

Dress B

Diag 45

Diag 46

Sleeve for Dress B

Diag 47 Wide Puffed Sleeve

thirtythree

Dress B

Diag 45 shows block pattern with straight line running from shoulder to bottom of dress.

Broken line at shoulder is for suppression to give shape over bust.

Broken line outside shoulder and armhole is for allowance of quantity of suppression.

Shoulder at point 15 can be extended 1¼" to give dropped shoulder effect (as Dress B shows). In this case we reduce sleeve head 1¼" at 0 to nothing at 3 as Diag 47 shows.

Cut out pattern in usual way and through broken lines.

Use top pattern for your dress fronts and shape neck 0 to 4.

Lay your patterns on to your material adding seam allowance of $\frac{3}{8}$" all through lines A and B and 3" each side at bottom to give width as broken lines indicate. More may be allowed to give extra fullness. Diag 46 shows where to cut your material along broken lines.

Sleeves and collar are cut as instructed on pages 16, 17, 30 and 31.

Centre front of neck at 4 should be cut open down to approx 3".

Block Pattern for Girls and Boys Coats

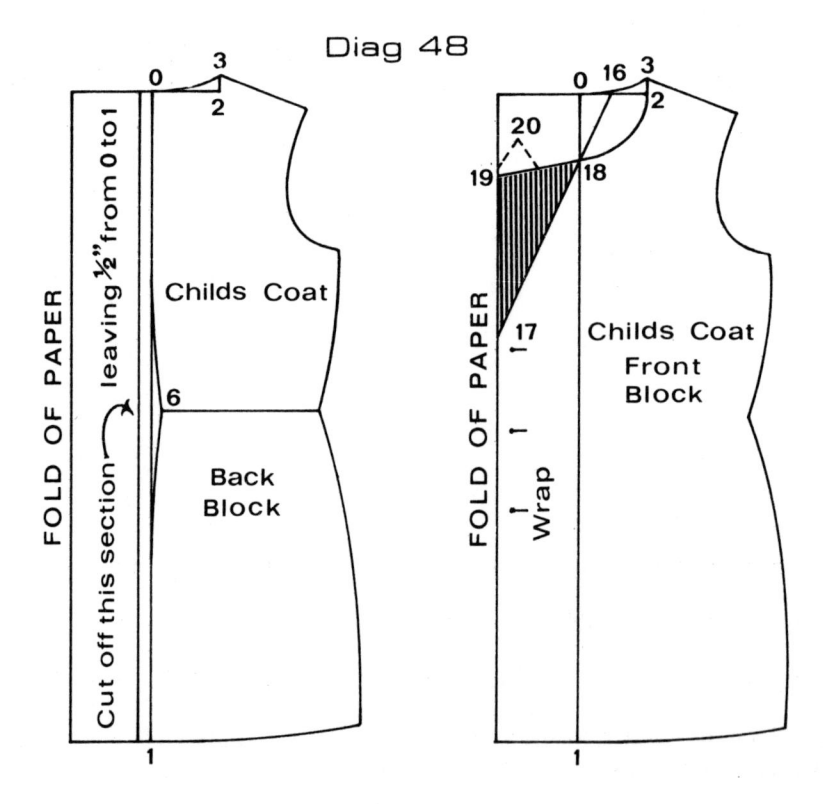

Diag 48

Block Pattern for Girls and Boys Coats

Always add 2½" above normal measurements at bust, waist and hips and 1" on cross back.

Use double sheet of paper as for dress. 0 to 1 line should be drawn 3" from front fold of paper for double breasted coat or 1¼" for single breasted coat, this section is for wrap of coat as diag 48 shows.

Mark out pattern as for dress, plus increased measurements, using half bust measurement for your scale.

Front darts can be added for a shaped coat.

Cut out pattern and cut through front fold of paper.

When cutting double breasted coat take under pattern and cut off 2½" at centre back from 0 to 1 and only cut off ¾" when cutting single breasted coat.

Take top section which is your front pattern.

16 is 1" from 3.

17 is position for top button which is any part of front edge you choose.

Run line from 16 to 17. This is your crease edge of lapel.

18 is 2½" from 0.

Shape through 3 – 2 – 18 to front edge at 19. Shaded section is lapel. This can be made wider or narrower to suit your desired taste by reducing or widening at 19 and running to 17.

Dotted line at 20 can be added for Double Breasted lapels.

Cut around neck 3 – 2 – 18 to 19 for Single Breasted lapel or around dotted line for Double Breasted lapel.

Cut two piece sleeves for coat as instructions on pages 40 – 41 and **always** take measurement around armhole of pattern to get correct size of sleeve head.

Coat under collar is cut as instructions on pages 42 and 43, measure around neck for correct size from 0 to 3 of back and 3 – 2 – 18 to 1¼" from front edge of lapel where collar should finish. This completes coat block pattern for both Girls or Boys.

Mark Stitching

Diag 49

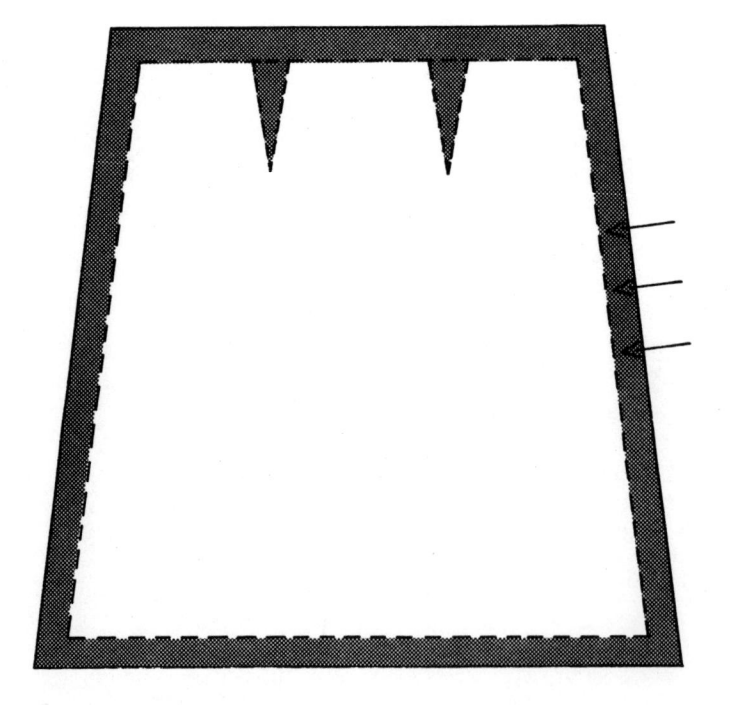

thirtyfive

Mark Stitching

After your garment is cut, and before making up, mark stitch all inlays. This is to show your edge line when sewing seams. This is done with needle and double basting thread — thread to be of a different colour to the material you are making up.

Each stitch should be approximately 2" apart.

Diagram 49 shows how this should be done. Broken lines indicate marking stitches. Shaded parts are inlays.

All marking stitches should be cut in the centre as indicated by arrows in diagram 49.

Before separating your material you cut your mark stitches between the two layers. When this is done your garment is now ready to baste for a fitting, using mark stitches as your guide lines.

Sewing Your Skirt

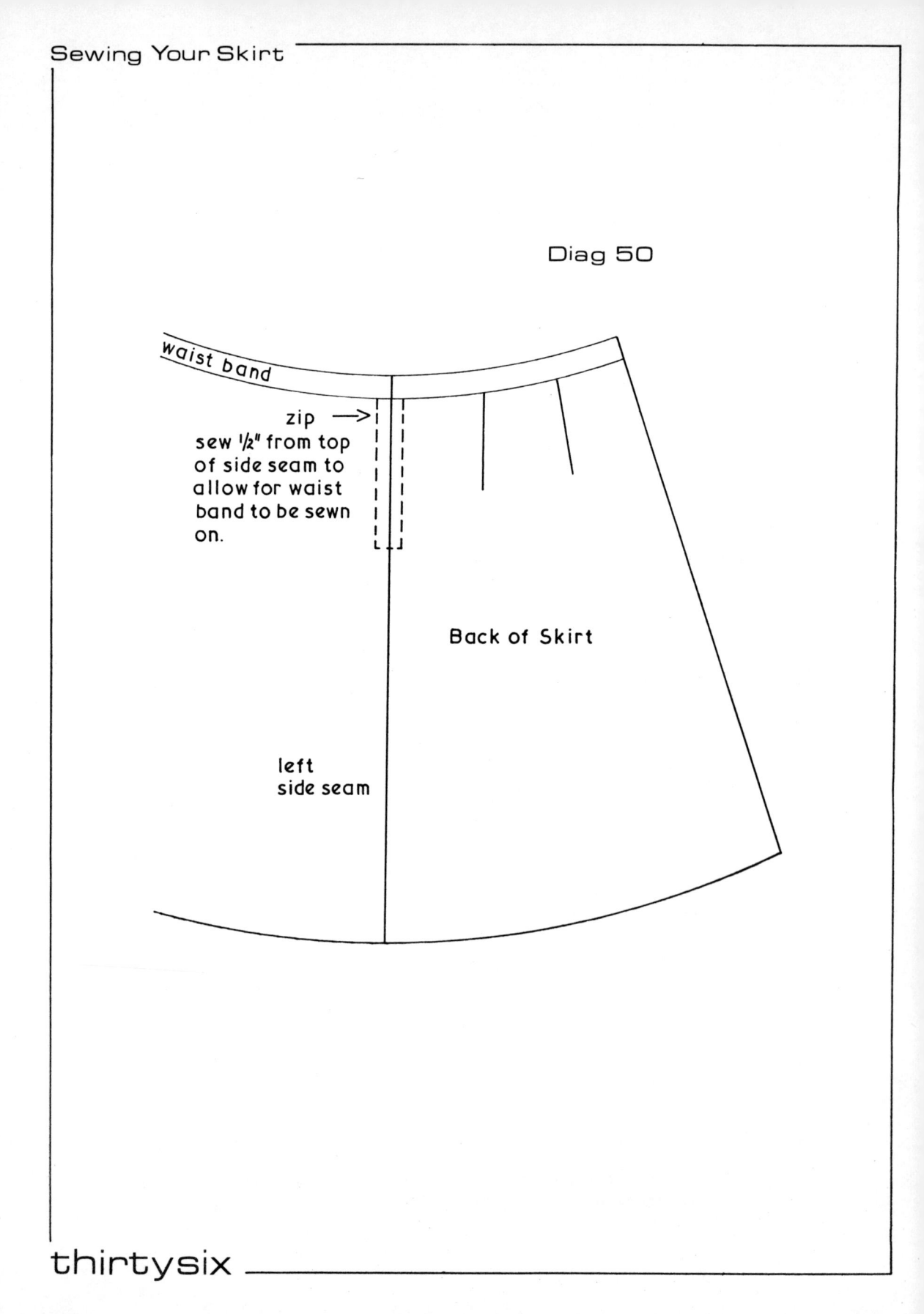

Diag 50

waist band

zip →
sew ½" from top of side seam to allow for waist band to be sewn on.

Back of Skirt

left side seam

thirtysix

Skirt Making

Diagram 7 on Page 24 is a close fitting skirt. Mark stitches are not required at side seams as there are no side seam inlays allowed. The only mark stitches necessary are for back darts numbers 8 — 9 and down to 11. Also at bottom for the length and for the position of zip at 7 down to 4 but coming in ½" into skirt at 4 as that is where your side seam starts. You may also allow inlays at side seams when cutting, if this is done then you do mark stitch side seams.

If you wish to line your skirt, linings should be cut identical to your skirt but 1½" shorter than your skirt length. For a pleated skirt lining should end at top of pleats.

If a cloth waistband is required this is cut 2" longer than your natural waist measurement to allow for turning in at both ends and should be cut approximately 3¼" wide. A fusible interlining for the waistband will give a nice firm finish to waist line. This should be cut 1" narrower than your waistband and pressed on ½" away from edges. When a 3¼" waistband is sewn on it will only be 1¼" wide when finished as this is folded back in the centre and ⅜" seams are sewn. A more simple way of making up the waist is by using a stiff petersham instead of a waistband. This is done by basting back a seam all around the top of waist line of the skirt and basting petersham to inside of waist of skirt then sewing on at the top edge only, a hook and eye should be sewn on at end of waist above zip.

Basting Skirt for Fitting

Back and front of skirt should be opened out as diagram 7a Page 24 and laid on top of each other — wrong side of cloth facing out. Skirt is now ready for basting. Baste from 7 to 6 down to bottom of hem. ⅜" wide seams should be taken all through, though we allow ½" for seams the extra ⅛" for ease which all materials will require.

Now baste ⅜" from edge at 4 down to bottom of skirt, baste up back darts through mark stitches 8 and 9 down to 11.

When this is completed turn your skirt right side out, and baste up bottom of hem the correct side in.

Zip section from 12 to 13 should be turned in and basted at 7 down to side seam at 4. A 7" zip should now be basted into this section and your skirt is now ready for fitting.

The skirt can be fitted without the waistband, it is not necessary to baste it on until after the garment has been fitted and any adjustments have been made and completely sewn up.

If you are lining the skirt, any adjustments that have been made at the fitting of skirt should also be carried out on the lining.

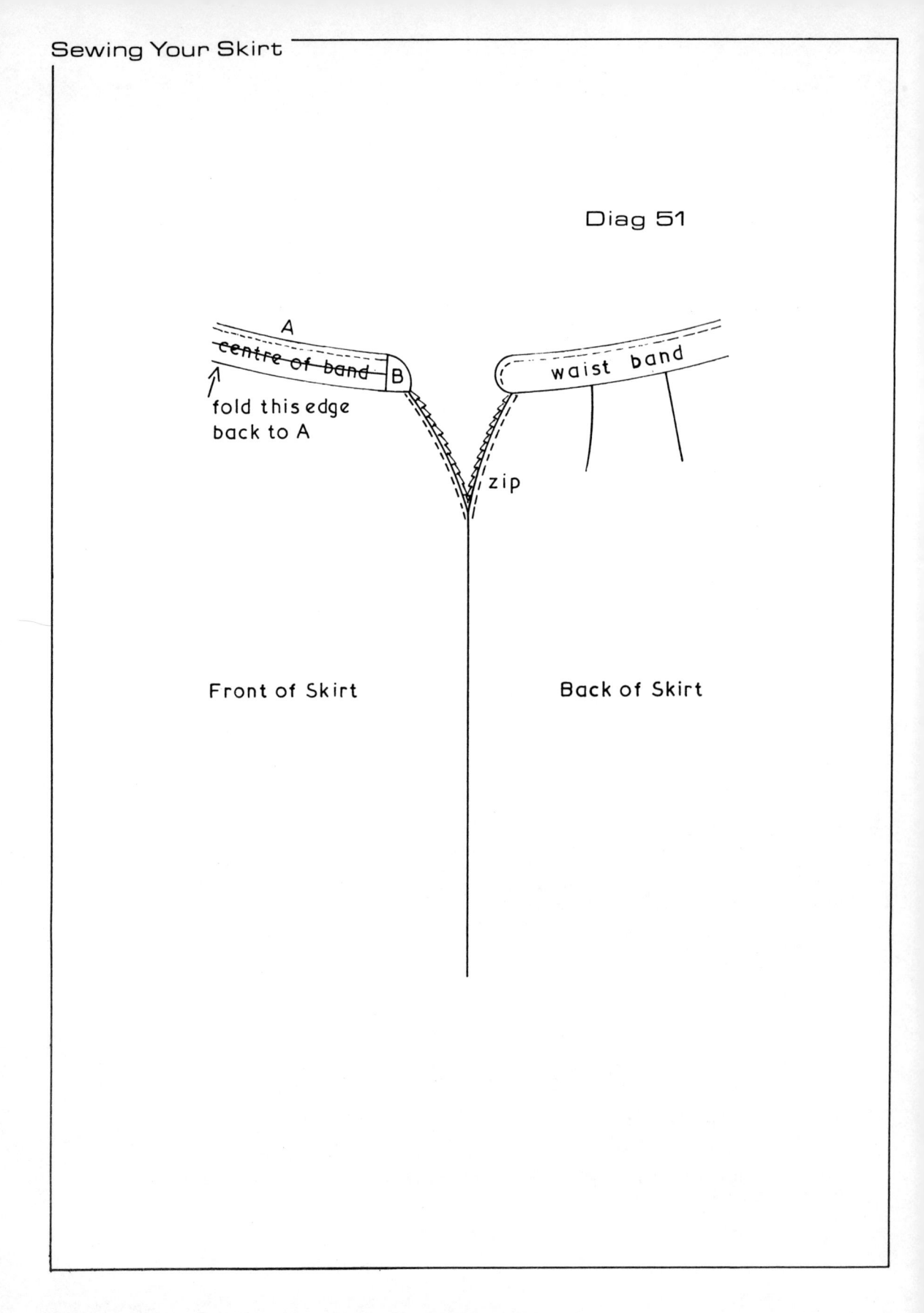

Sewing Your Skirt

Diag 51

A
centre of band
B
fold this edge back to A

waist band

zip

Front of Skirt

Back of Skirt

Sewing Your Skirt

Remove zip from skirt to allow machine to sew your seams, then machine your side seams and darts and press open all seams and darts. Baste in zip starting ½" from top at 7 down to 4 (diagram 50 shows zip sewn into left side seam) now sew on zip ⅜" from edge either by hand or machine.

After the zip is sewn in, you sew up your linings the same as the skirt and turn up hem of lining. When this is complete you baste the lining into the skirt all around the waist line — the raw edge of lining to the raw edge of waist of skirt, then turn in lining ⅜" away from edge of zip and sew around by hand.

When this is completed you baste waistband on to top of skirt as diagram 51 at A. Machine on waistband as broken line shows folding back 1" at B and extending 1" at C shaded section. When this is sewn on you fold waistband in halves as diagram 51 and sew down inside. In doing this you have also sewn in your lining around your waist line.

A hook and eye should be sewn on at edge of B and C.

Bottom of skirt hem should be bound with skirt binding and then sewn on with a very fine stitch so as not to show through outside.

Apart from pressing, your skirt is now finished. Pressing should be done on a sleeve board or domestic pressing board.

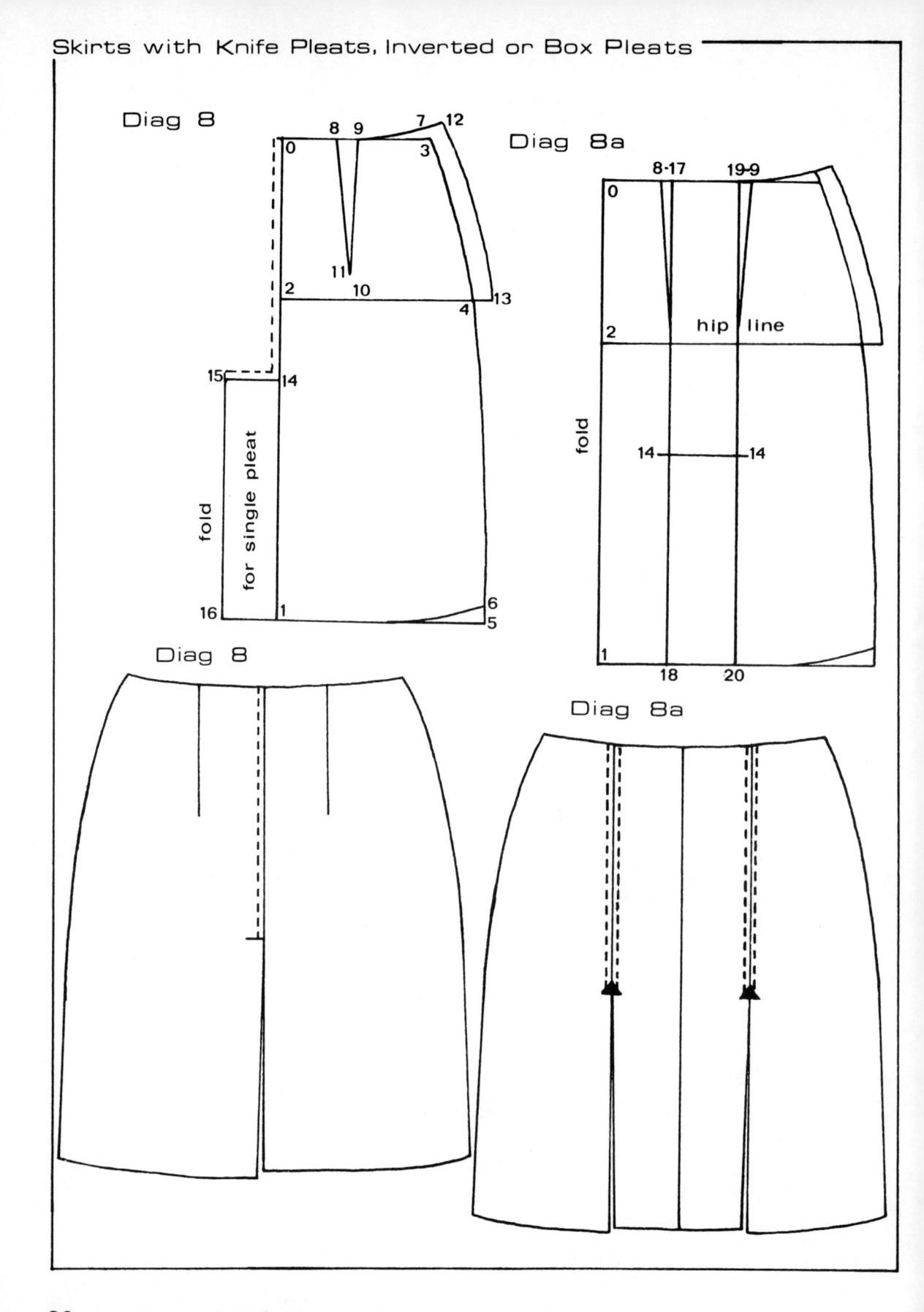

Skirts with Knife Pleats, Inverted or Box Pleats

Diag 8

Diag 8a

Making Skirts with either Knife, Box or Inverted Pleats

These are made in the same way as a plain skirt. For a Knife Pleat as diagram 8 Page 26 shows sew your seam from 0 to 14 and press over to one side from 0 down to 1 at bottom of skirt. You may top stitch your seam from 0 to 14 as diagram 8 Page 26 shows. Broken line is your stitching.

For a Box Pleat skirt you do the same as for a Knife Pleat, the only difference is that you press the seams over to the centre of your garment from top to bottom of skirt from 8 to 18 as top diagram 8a. Top stitch your seam from 8 to 14 and across 14 to hold pleat.

For Inverted Pleats as diagram 8a bottom, sew your seams from 8 down to 14 and press open. The pleats start at 14 and should be pressed half way to centre of skirt and half to side seams. Lower diagram 8A shows where Inverted Pleats should be stitched, broken line indicates machine stitching.

Pleats should be made before basting your side seams for fitting of skirt.

Making a Dress

Diag 52

thirtyseven

Making a Dress

After your garment is cut, marking stitches should be put in your inlays.

Baste your dress for fitting. It is not necessary to baste in the collar or sleeves until you have fitted your garment and made any adjustments, as sometimes the armholes may want easing. Once you are satisfied with the fitting of your dress it should now be sewn.

When this is done you baste your collar and sleeves into dress for a further fitting. If everything fits correctly you can now complete your garment or make any further adjustments if necessary.

When making a dress with a collar or revers it is advisable to use a fusible interlining which should be pressed on to the inside of the material.

Fusible interlining can be bought at most shops and stores when purchasing your materials. Your suppliers will also advise you on what kind of fusible interlining would be most suitable for the material you have chosen.

Should you wish to line your dress, cut the lining the same as your dress. Linings should be 1½" shorter than your dress.

If you have made any adjustments to your dress after fitting, alter the lining in the same way so as they are both the same.

To sew lining in dress sew all seams in lining and baste lining around the neck and armholes. Before finishing neck, sew in collar and sleeves.

When sewing sleeves into garment, a certain amount of easing into armhole or gathering is required around the crown of sleeve — diagram 3 Page 16 crown is from 5 to 0 on to 6. Before sewing sleeve into armhole measure distance around armhole, then measure sleeve head from 3 to 5 on to 0 to 6 and back to 3. Sleeve head should measure approximately 1½" more than armhole to allow for ease. If sleeve head measures over 1½" more than armhole this can be reduced as follows: diagram 52 shows sleeve head from 3 to 0. Broken line shows where sleeve is reduced. Place tape measure at point A of sleeve which is ¼" below normal sleeve head and reduce sleeve seam at 3 broken line so that sleeve measures the required size from 0 to 3.

To baste sleeves into armholes match point 3 of sleeve to point 5 of dress diagram 1 Page 16, and 0 of sleeve to 15 of dress. Be sure to use right sleeve for right armhole.

Before sewing in sleeves, dress should be fitted once more to make certain sleeves hang correctly and dress length is even before finishing. Where hand finishing is required use a fine needle and cotton, or sylko, to prevent any stitches from showing on the outside.

Trouser Making

Diag 53

Trouser Making

Mark stitch all inlays that have been allowed and always the bottoms for correct length.

When these have been cut through separate your materials and place front section to back section at point 4 diagram 21 Page 46 to point 12 diagram 22 Page 48.

Make sure the wrong side of your materials is facing outside.

Baste inside leg 4 and 12 down to 9 and 15.

Baste back darts 21 — 22 down to 24.

Baste outside leg seams from 3 down to 10 and from 4 to 0 and 12 to 19.

The zip should now be basted in at top of left side seam in the same way as for a skirt.

If a fly front zip is required, when cutting trousers instead of allowing 1½" of material at 20 to 3 this should be added at 0 to 6 for zip to be sewn into the material.

Outside leg seam should be basted from top at 1 down to 10.

Bottoms of trousers should now be basted to required length.

Trousers are now ready for fitting.

After fitting and making any adjustments that are sometimes necessary the trousers can now be sewn up.

A cloth or petersham waistband can now be added in the same way as for a skirt.

The bottoms of trousers should be sewn by hand using a fine needle with a fine matching cotton or sylko, the latter for preference. Do not hold stitches tight otherwise this may show on the outside.

Press open seams and darts before pressing creases into shape.

To press front and back creases the trousers should be laid flat on ironing board and should be pressed flat from top through 7 down to 11, as diagram 53, pressing one leg at a time, with outside leg seam and inside leg seam on top of each other. It is adviseable to use either a steam iron or damp press cloth with temperature of iron on steam, as this will give a firm crease and smooth finish to your trousers.

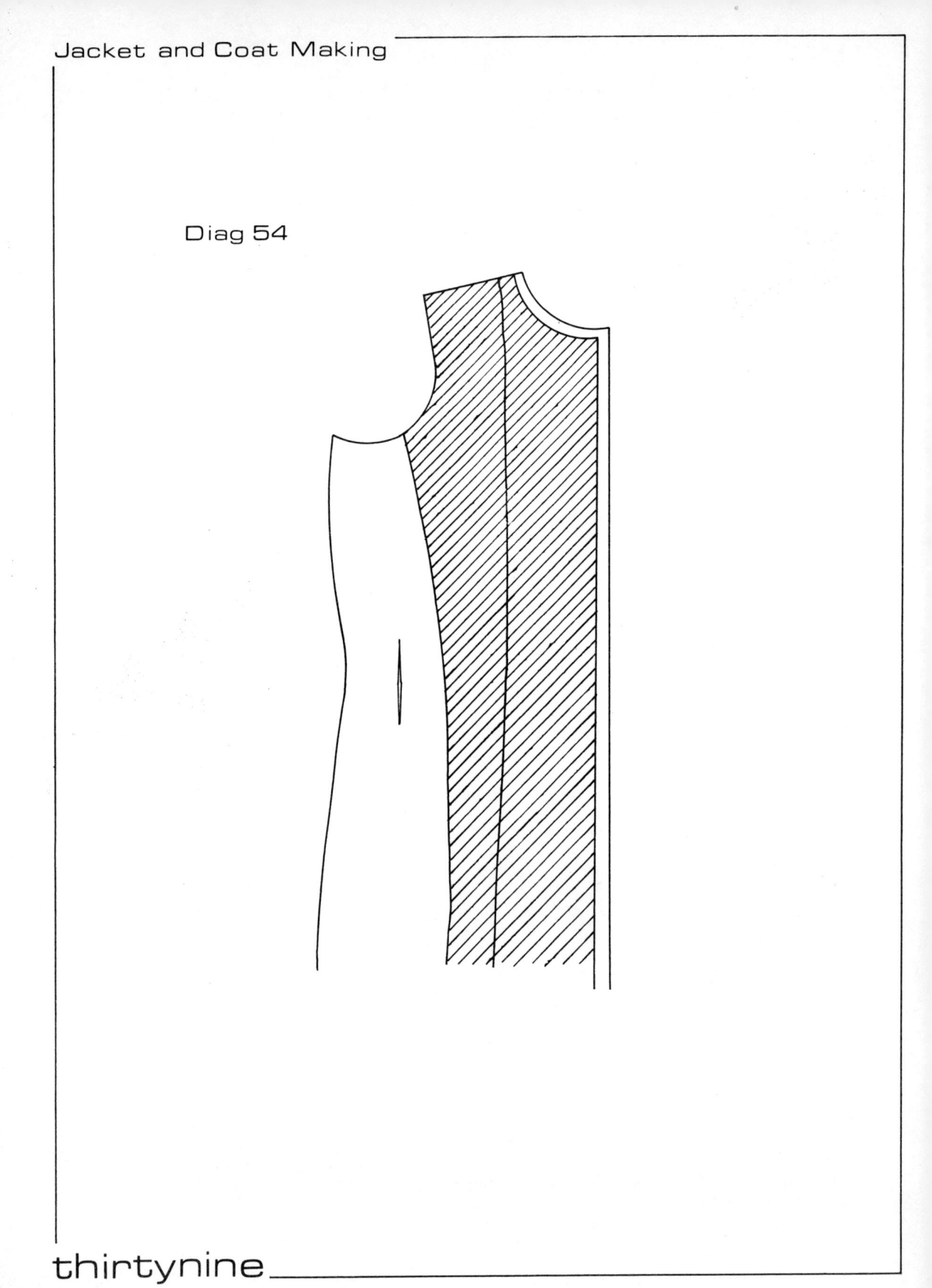

Jacket and Coat Making

Diag 54

thirtynine

Jacket and Coat Making

When making a coat or jacket, linings and canvas should be cut before sewing your garment. It is adviseable to canvas fronts and revers as this will give the garment a firm and professional finish.

The type of canvas used depends on the material you use for your garment. When buying your material your supplier will advise you on the correct canvas to use.

Canvasses should be cut the same shape as your garment fronts and basted on after sewing and pressing open any seams that have been cut in garment fronts.

Diagram 54 shows fronts with diagonal lines representing canvas.

Cut canvas ¼" away from the edges of your coat.

Coat facings should be machined on just away from edge of canvas, this will give a fine thin edge to the garment.

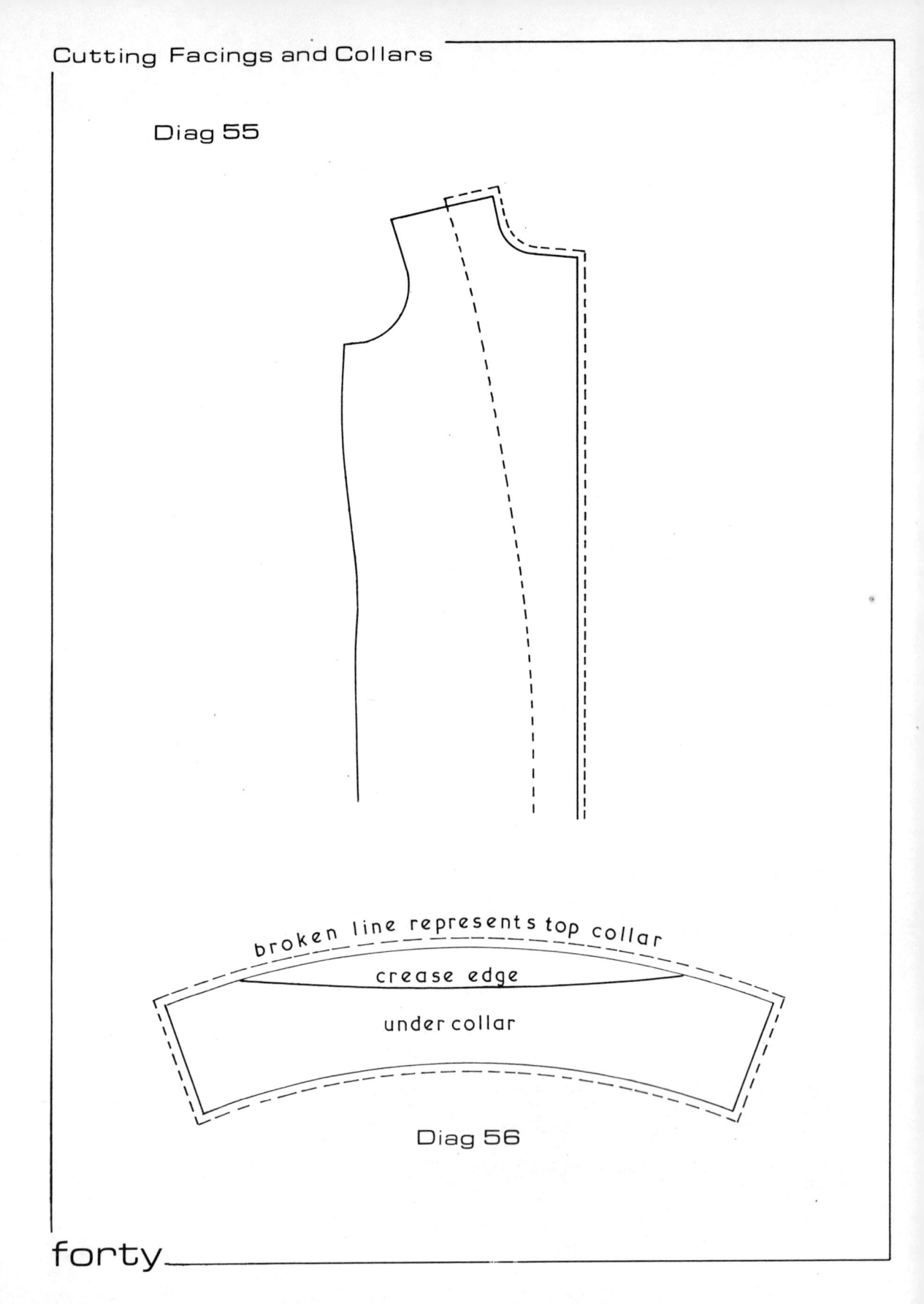

Cutting Facings and Collars

Diag 55

broken line represents top collar

crease edge

under collar

Diag 56

forty

Cutting Facings and Collars

Facings should be cut the same size as fronts of garment plus ¼" wider all around to allow for ease. Diagram 55 shows facings at broken lines. Top collar should be cut ⅛" longer and wider than under collar and should be in one piece. The extra size of top collar is to allow for ease when covering collar as diagram 56.

If your garment is to be lined, linings should be cut the same size as your jacket or coat plus ½" on the double at the centre back and ¼" at the side seams. The lining for the fronts should be cut the same way less the width of your facing plus ¾" on the fronts for sewing on to the facings.

If pockets are required, the position should be marked on your garment at the time of fitting as you may want to shorten or lengthen your garment, and accordingly you will either have to raise or lower your pockets.

Pocket Making

Diag 57

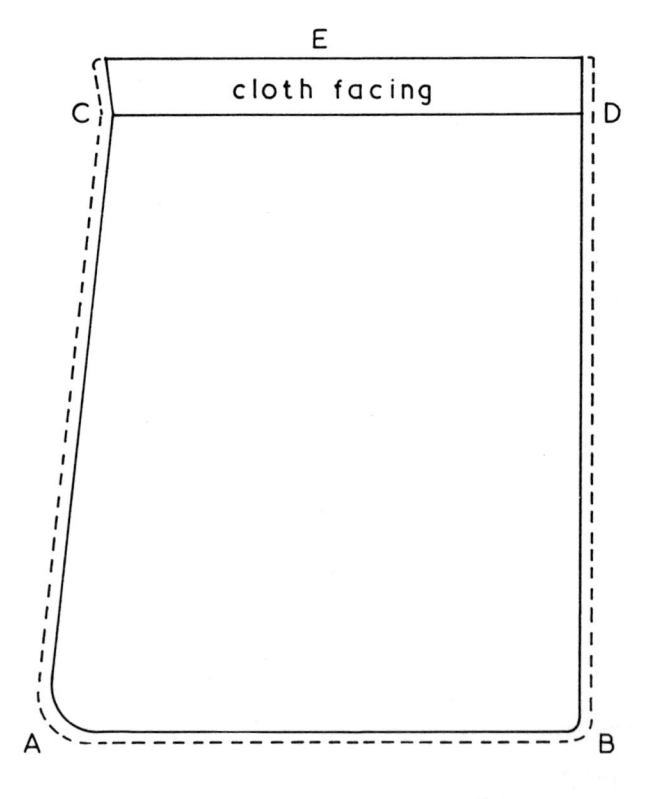

```
         E
   C ┌─cloth facing─┐ D
     │              │
     │              │
     │              │
     │              │
     │              │
   A └──────────────┘ B
```

fortyone

Pocket Making

There are several types of pockets that one can make.

Patch pockets or patch and flap. Jetted pockets or jetted and flap. Flap only or jetted only or welted pockets.

For patch pockets decide on the size of the patch you wish to make leaving an extra ¼" all around for seams at a, b, c and d, and 1" extra on the top for facings as diagram 57. Round the corners slightly at a and b. Patches should be lined. Cut your lining the same size as your patch less ⅛" at side at a and b to the same width as patch at c and d.

Lining should be sewn across top of patch at e leaving a 2" opening in centre as diagram 58 shows.

Lining and facing should now be folded over at F as diagram 59. Diagonal lines indicate facing at top of pockets, broken lines indicate lining.

Be certain when folding at F the outside should now be the wrong side of material. Baste around edges from top at C to A — B and D holding lining slightly tight across from A to B. This will prevent lining showing through at side when sewn onto garment. Now machine your lining onto patch, sewing where basted. You then turn your pocket out, pushing it through the 2" opening at E. When this is done get your corners pulled out nice and slightly rounded by using the tip of your needle to pull the corners through.

Baste your patch all around the edges before pressing as diagram 60 then fell stitch the 2" opening at the top of lining at E diagram 60.

Now you press your patch and place it in position on your garment and baste it on. This is now ready for sewing on either by hand or machine.

Patch pocket with flap. Make your patch pocket as instructed and sew on to your garment. Then cut a piece of material 1" longer than pocket from C to D diagram 59.

The width of flap is your own choice although the average is between 2¼" and 3". Cut your lining the same size less ⅛" all round and baste on to cloth flap holding lining slightly on the tight side, be sure the cloth is the wrong side out. Diagram 61 is the flap.

Now machine lining onto the flap from A — B — C to D, do not machine along top from A to D as diagram 61. Turn out and baste the same way as your patch and press. Baste flap 1" above patch with lining facing you and machine onto the garment from A to D as diagram 62 shows.

Fold over flap at B and C to top of patch. This should be top stitched across flap from A to D to cover the raw edge of flap. Diagram 63 shows complete patch with flap pocket.

Pocket Making

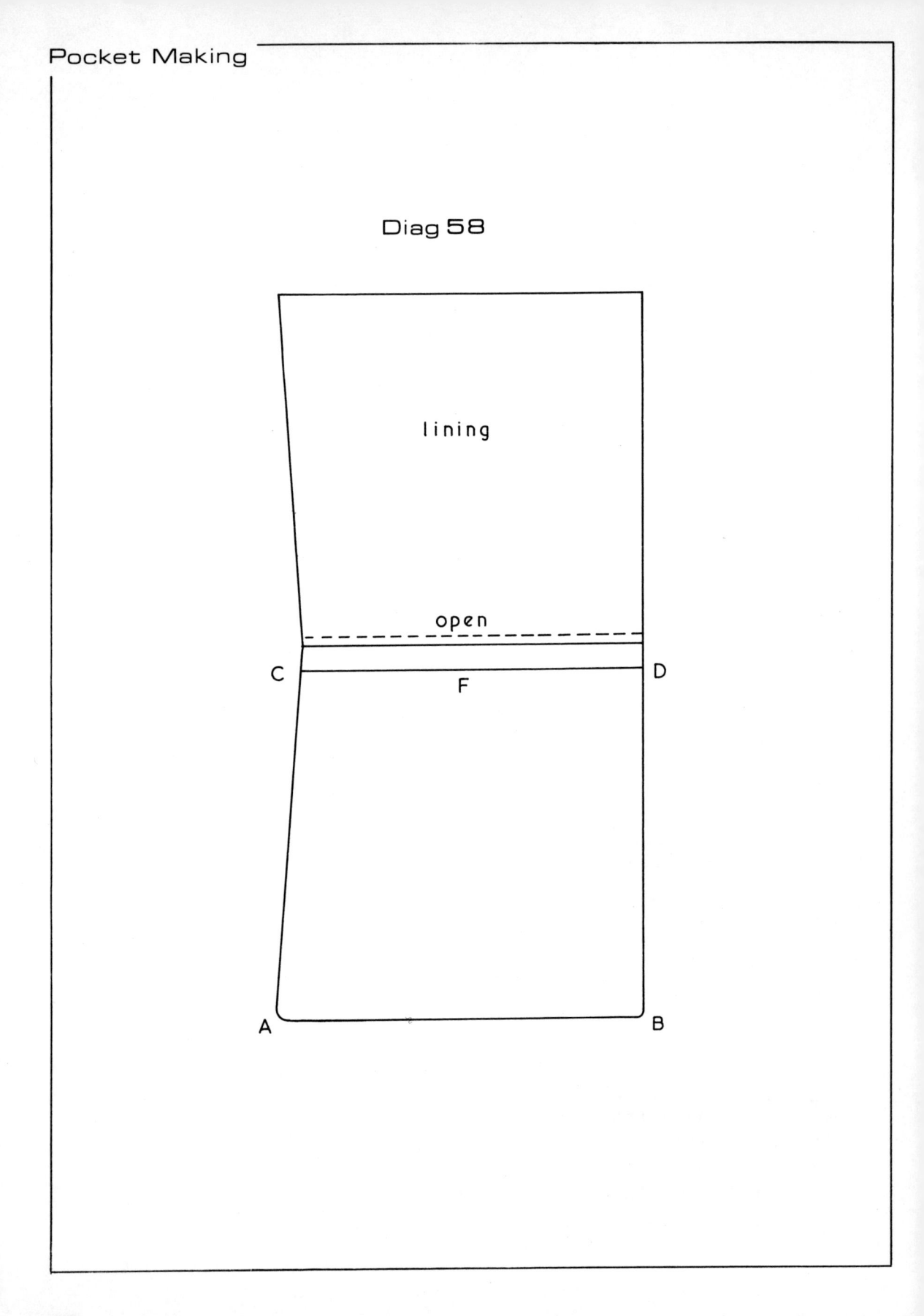

Diag 58

lining

open

C   F   D

A   B

Jetted pockets. Two strips of cloth are required for each pocket. Whatever width you decide your pocket to be cut two strips of materials 1½" longer than opening for pocket by 1½" in depth. Pocket linings should be approximately 6" in depth and measure the same across as your strips of cloth.

For each of your pockets one strip of cloth should be sewn on to one piece of pocket lining. Diagram 64 shows where lining should be sewn on to cloth, turning in raw edge of lining. When doing this the right side of cloth and lining should be facing you. Thick line on diagram 65 shows where pocket will be cut. Sew strip without lining on to top of thick line from A to B leaving ¾" of strip to extend at each end. Now sew the strip with the lining to bottom part of thick line from A to B also leaving ¾" of your strip at each end. After you have both strips sewn to garment you cut through your pocket stopping ¼" before A and B. Now cut a V shape at A and B as diagram 66. Turn garment over so that the wrong side of cloth faces you and press open seam of bottom section and press both V corners back, the left one over to the left and the right side over to the right. The top section of pocket should now be pulled through the opening and seam pressed open. Now pull through bottom section and baste ¼" jetts on right side of garment as diagram 67. When this is done, hand sew jetting through the seam from A to B with back stitching so that stitches do not show. Place your second piece of lining underneath your pocket and level with your top piece and sew all around your lining by machine, catching on the V sections and across the top of the pocket as close as possible to the top jetting seam, this will stop your pocket from gaping open.

Pockets with Jetts and Flaps. For this you make a jetted pocket in the usual way, but before you sew around your lining you make your flap in the same way as for patch pocket with flap, the only difference being that you allow an extra 1" at top of flap as diagram 68 diagonal lines indicate the 1" allowance. You complete your pocket as for jetted only but before you sew around your lining you slide your flap into the pocket as diagram 69 and baste flap into position with the 1" allowance on top of flap to go above jetting on the inside of pocket. You now sew all around your pocket lining and across the top of pocket in the same way as for jetted only and this will hold your flap in place and complete your pocket.

Welt Pockets. For welts you only require one piece of cloth for each pocket. Each piece of cloth should measure double the required depth of welt when finished plus ½" for seams. If welt is to measure ¾" when finished it should be cut 2". Whatever measurement you choose to make your pocket across add ½" for seams. Now cut your linings — two pieces for each pocket ¾" wider than your pocket measurement across.

Next you take your cloth for welt and fold in halves outside to be the wrong side of cloth and sew up both ends as diagram 70 at A and B then turn inside out. Place raw edge of cloth on to garment in position of pocket as diagram 71 broken lines are the raw edges. Place pocket lining edge on top of welt raw edge to raw edge as diagram 72 wavy lines are lining and sew across from A to B. Then place your other piece of pocket lining above A and B as diagram 73 indicates and sew from A to B.

Cut through pockets from A to B cutting a V shape at corners and push linings through opening. Welt should now be folded upwards and corners should be stitched down as diagram 74. Dotted lines show stitching. Sew around pockets linings and this completes your welt pocket.

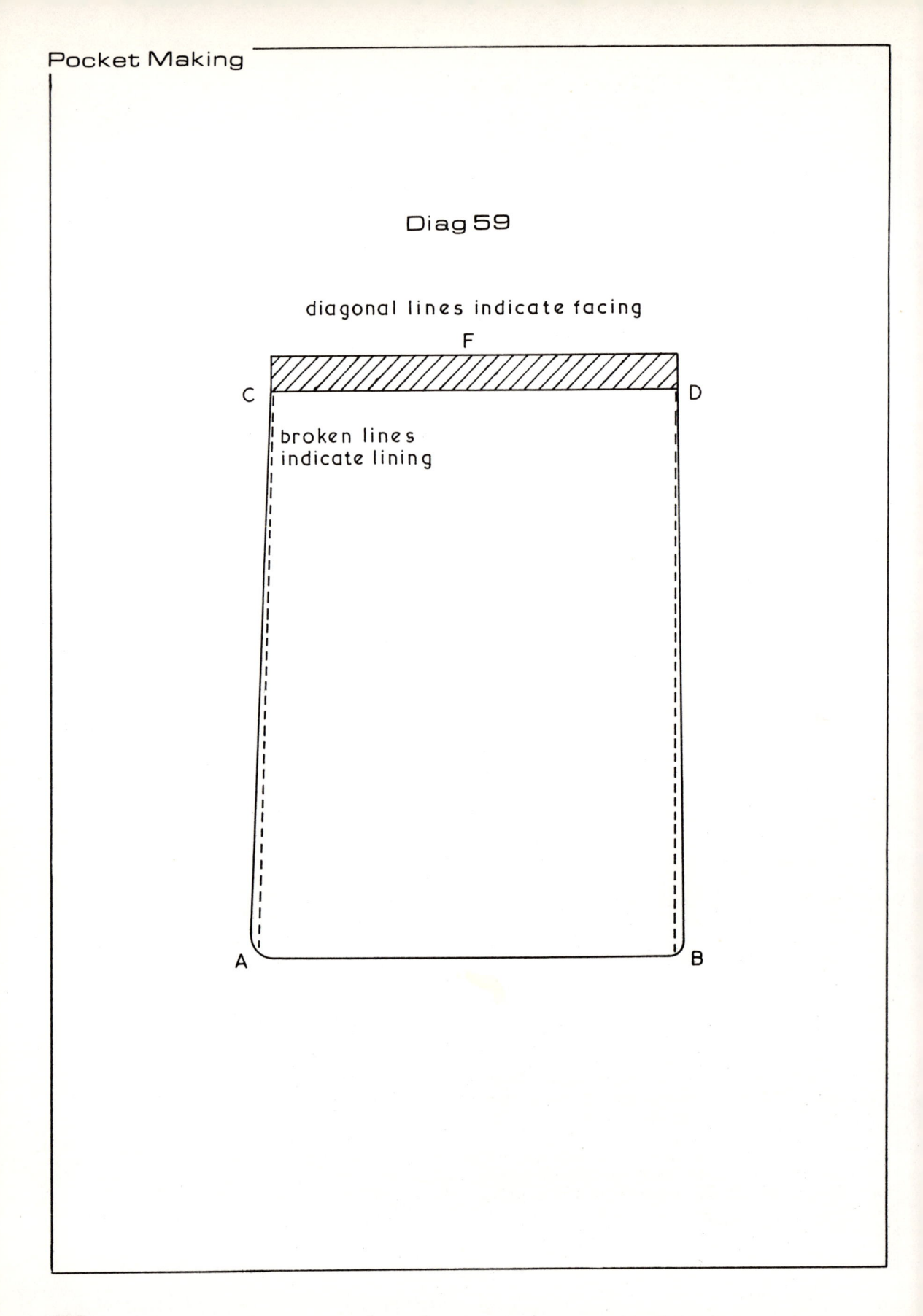

Pocket Making

Diag 59

diagonal lines indicate facing

broken lines indicate lining

Pocket Making

Diag 60

E

broken lines indicate
baste stitches all around
edge of patch pocket

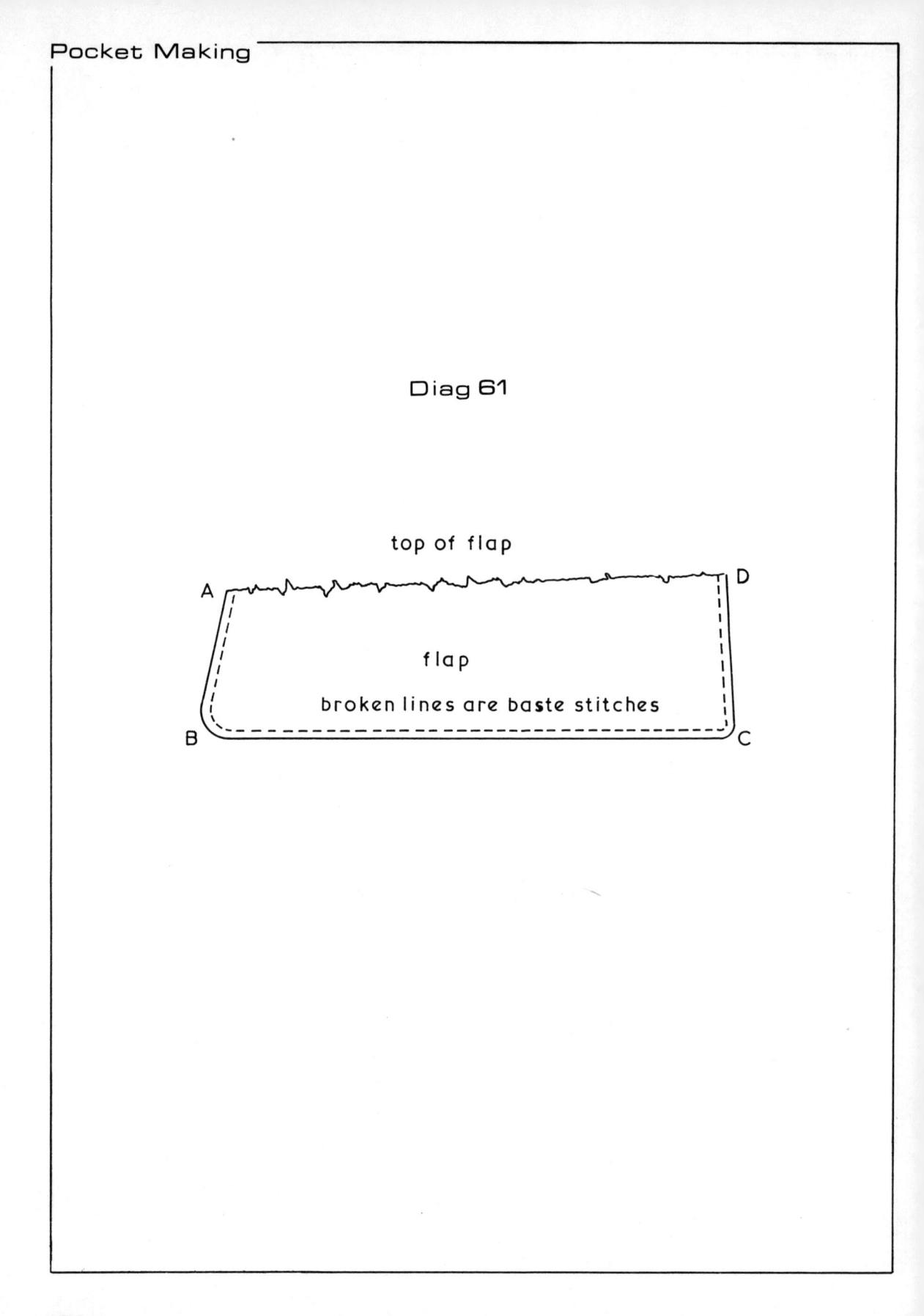

Pocket Making

Diag 61

top of flap

A D
flap
broken lines are baste stitches
B C

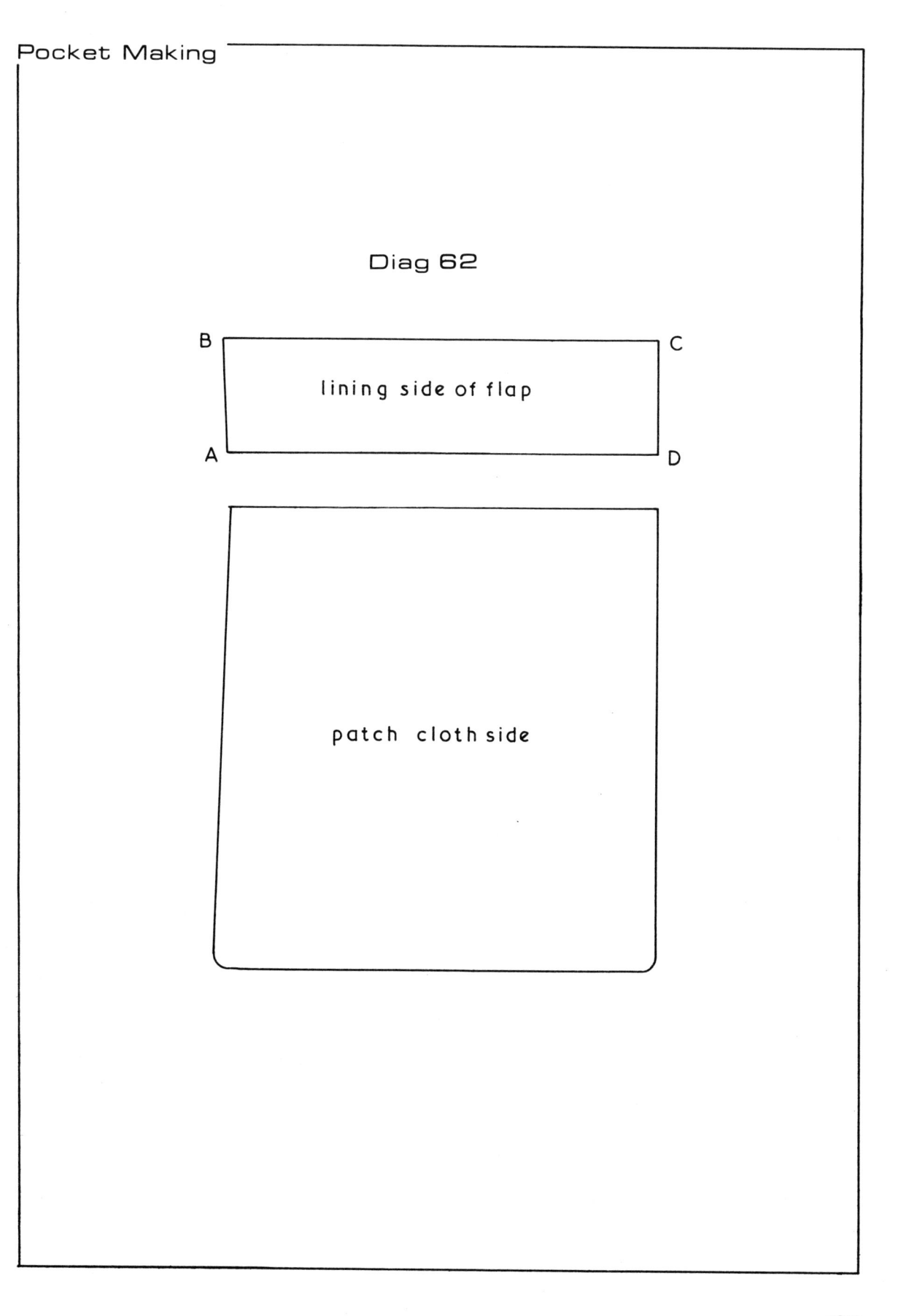

Pocket Making

Diag 62

B ┌──────────────────────────┐ C
  │   lining side of flap   │
A └──────────────────────────┘ D

patch cloth side

Pocket Making

patch pocket with flap

broken lines indicate where pocket
is sewn onto garment

Diag 63

Pocket Making

Diag 64

cloth facing

broken lines indicate machine stitching

Lining

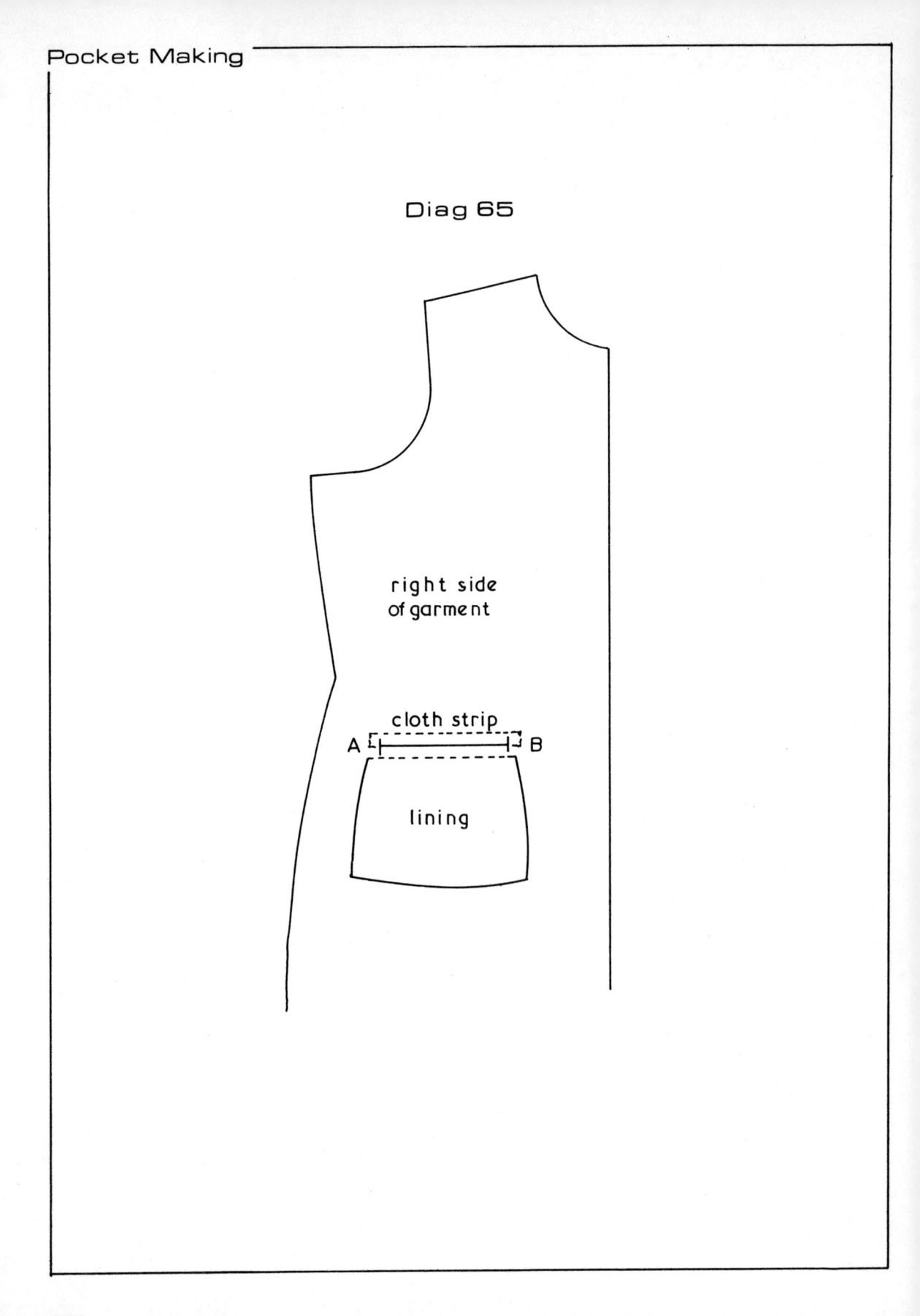

Pocket Making

Diag 65

right side
of garment

cloth strip

A   B

lining

106

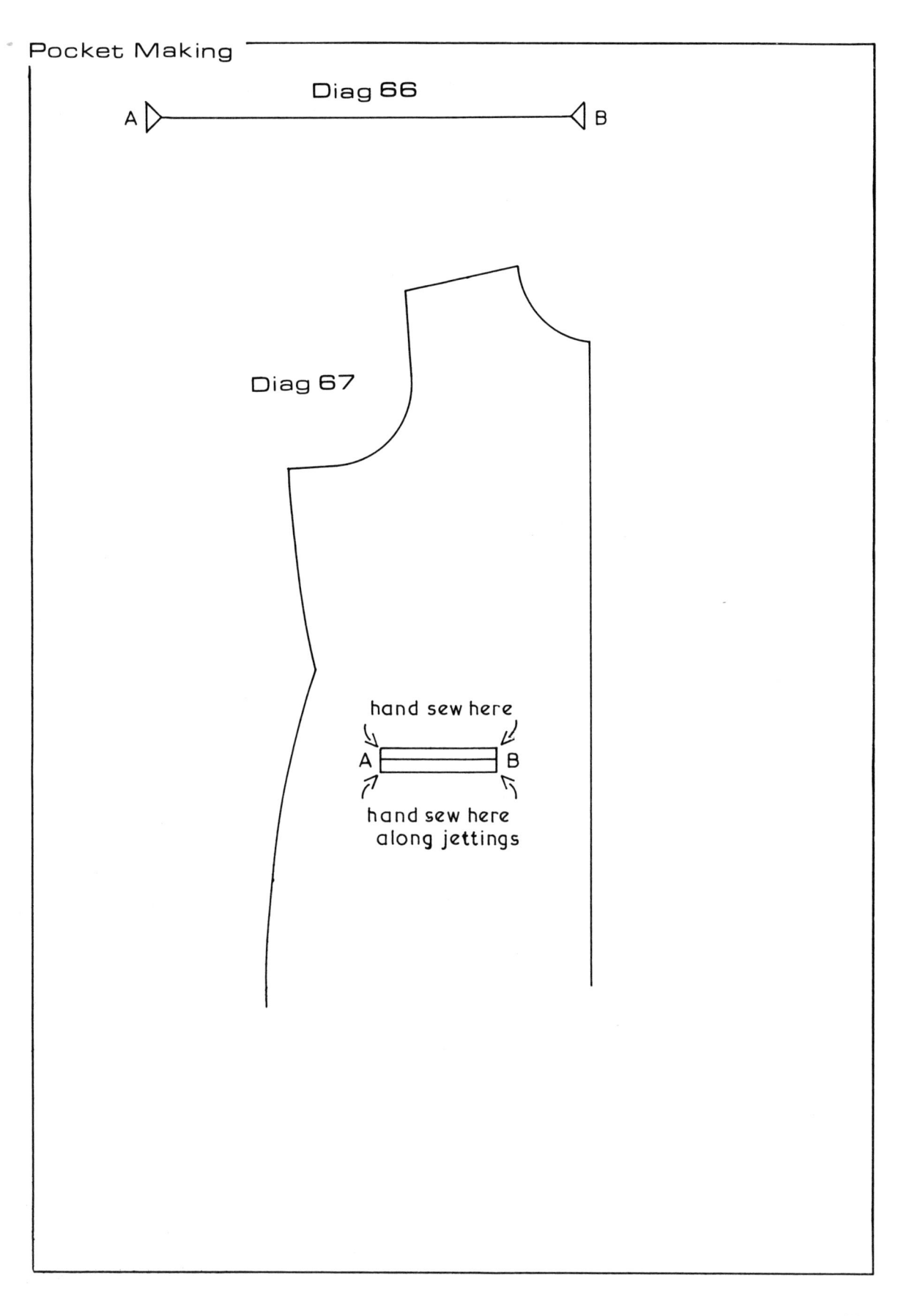

Pocket Making

Diag 66

A ▷—————————————◁ B

Diag 67

hand sew here

A [=======] B

hand sew here
along jettings

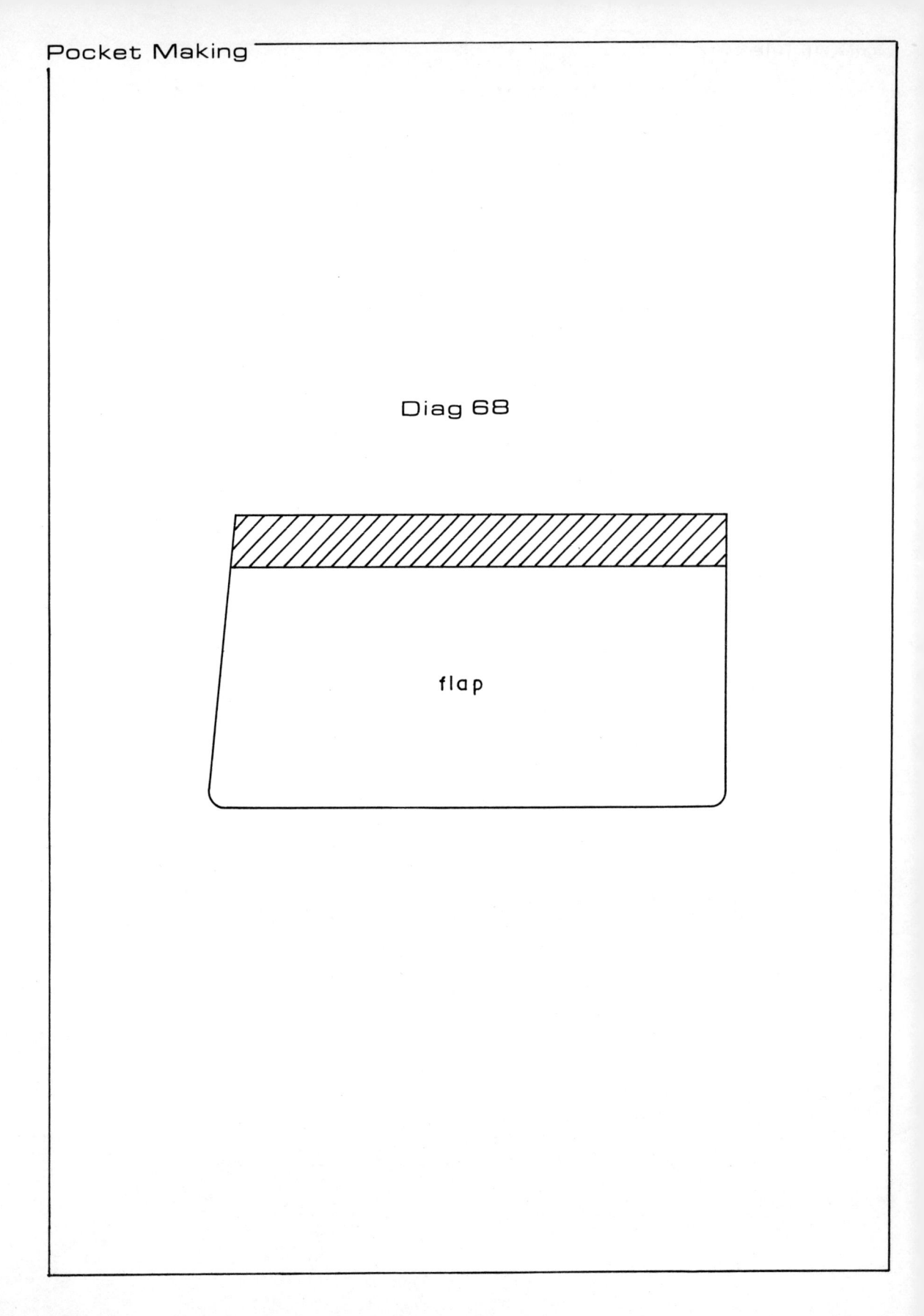

Pocket Making

Diag 68

flap

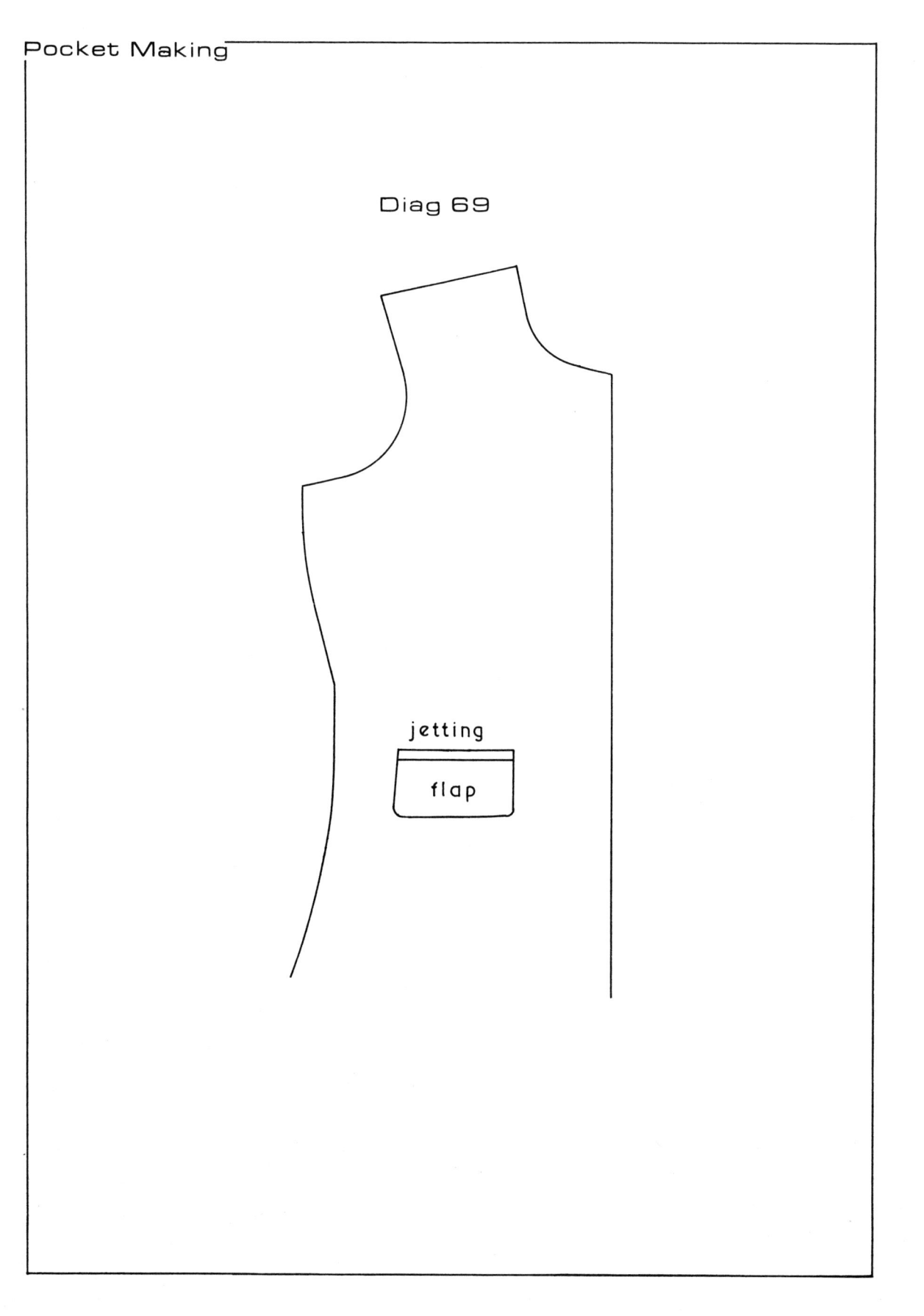

Pocket Making

Diag 69

jetting

flap

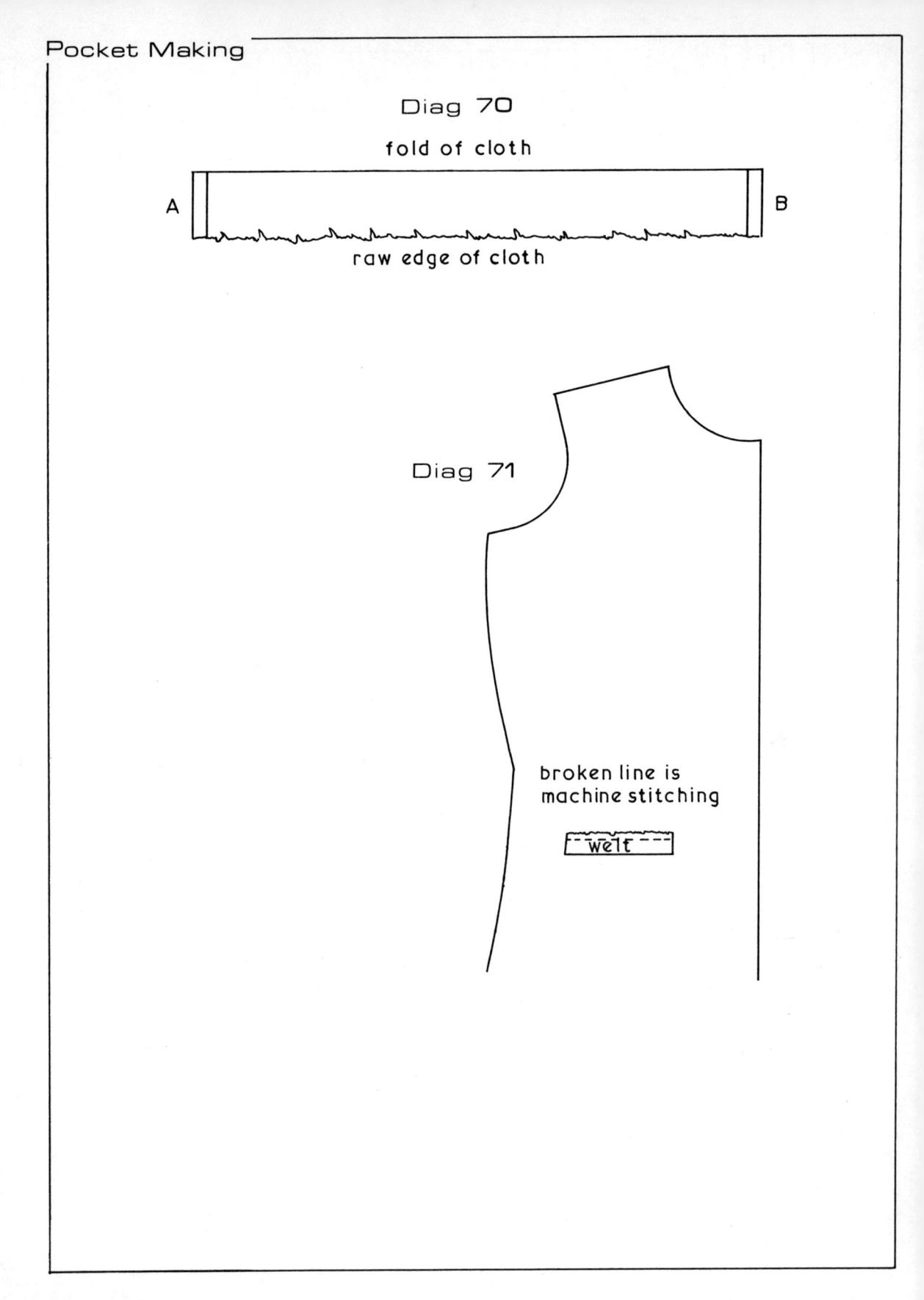

Pocket Making

Diag 70

fold of cloth

A ─────────────────── B

raw edge of cloth

Diag 71

broken line is machine stitching

welt

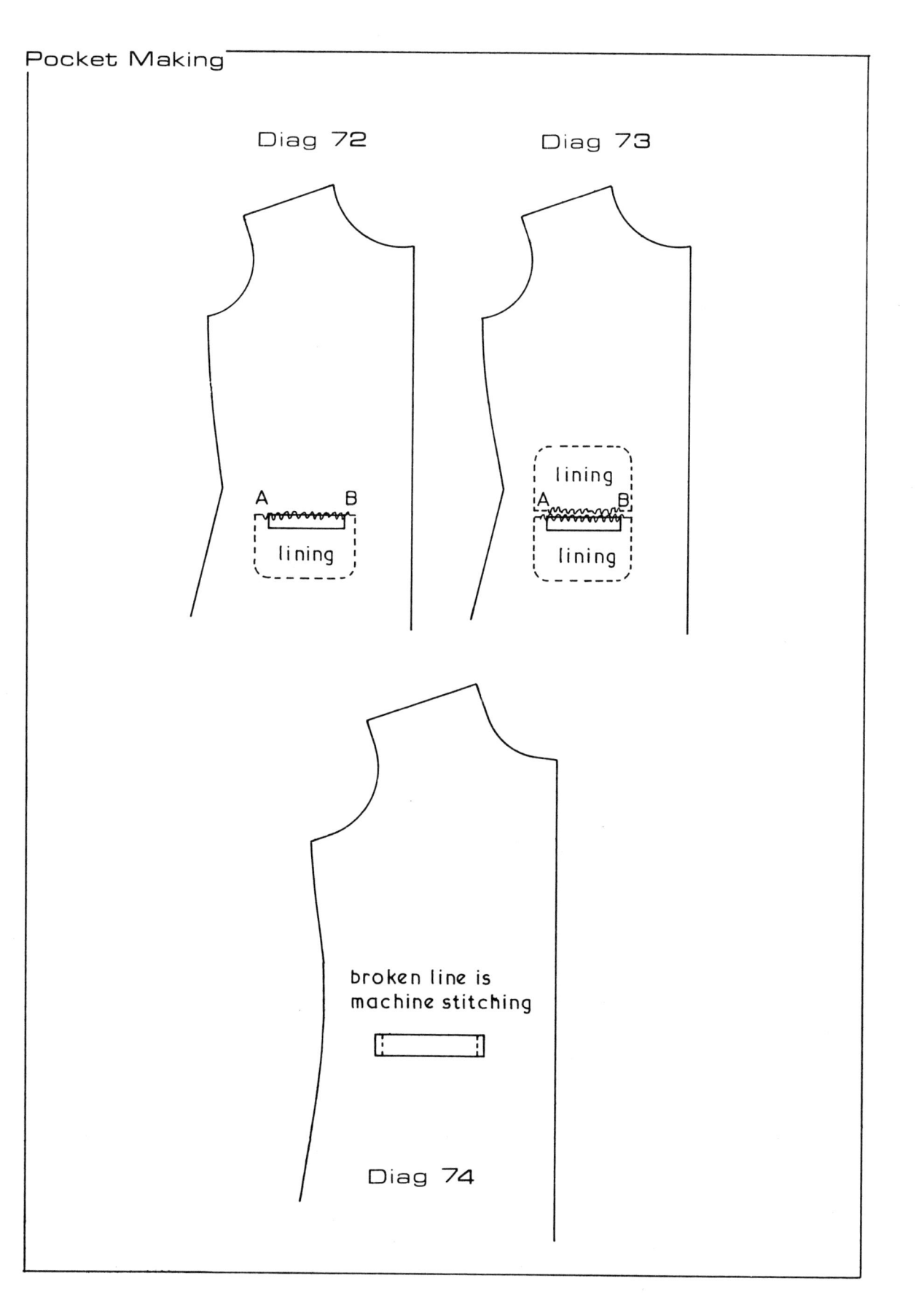

Pocket Making

Diag 72

Diag 73

A B
lining

A B
lining
lining

broken line is
machine stitching

Diag 74

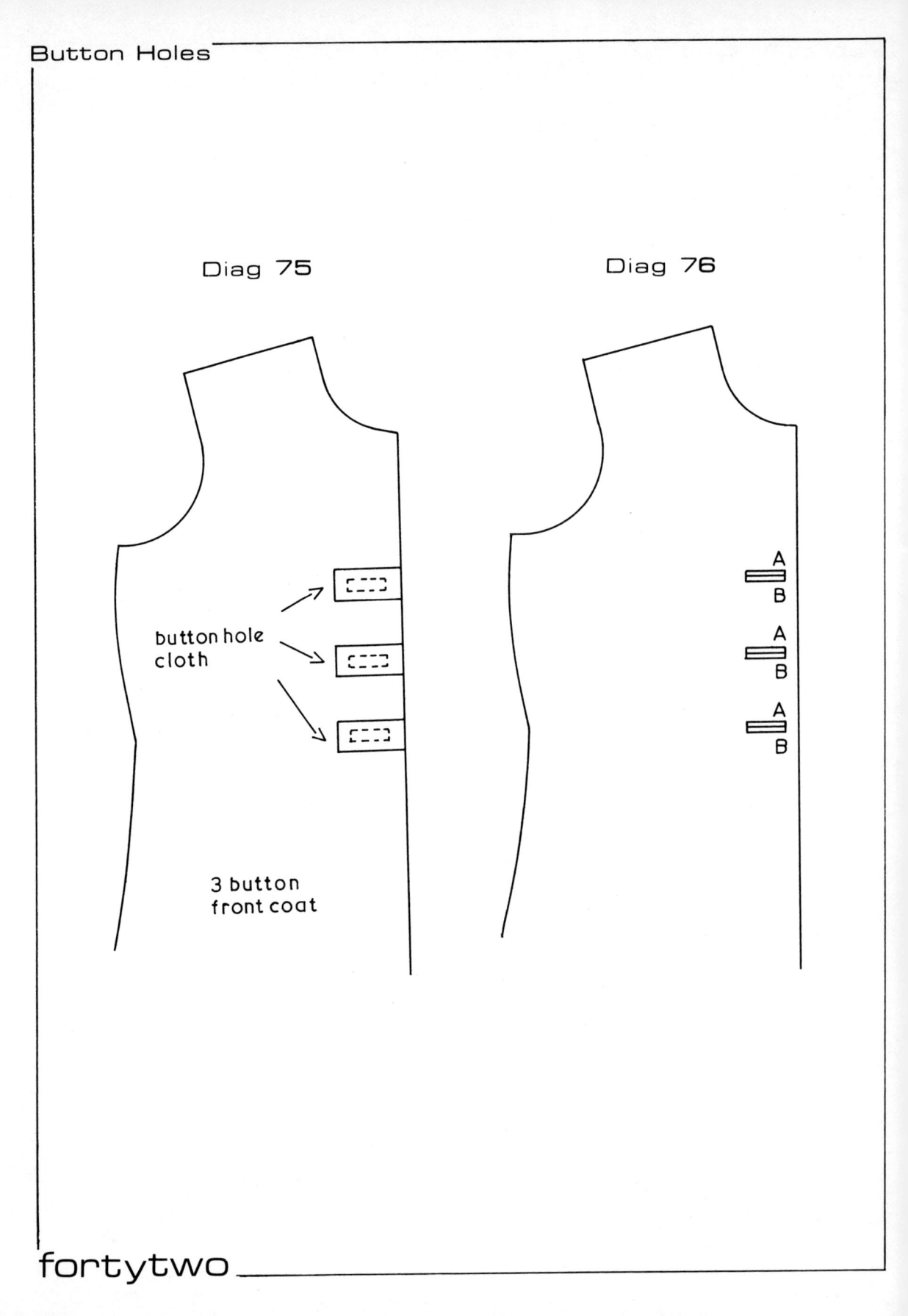

Button Holes

Diag 75

Diag 76

button hole cloth

3 button front coat

A B (×3)

fortytwo

Button Holes

There are two kinds of button holes explained here, those made with cloth and others that are made with button hole twist.

If you are making a cloth button hole in a garment that is to be interlined with canvas, the canvas must be put into the garment before making your holes and facings should not be put on until after holes are made.

Mark position and size of hole, then cut one piece of material for each hole 2¼" x 1" longer than the size of hole.

Place material over where hole is to be and machine onto garment as diagram 75 broken lines indicate machine stitching approximately ½" wide. Corners should be sewn straight not rounded. Cut through centre of stitching and push material through opening, making ¼" wide pipes each side, stitching by hand or machine through A and B as diagram 76. On completion of your garment cut through your facing at button hole openings and turn in raw edges and hand sew all around hole. This completes your piped button hole.

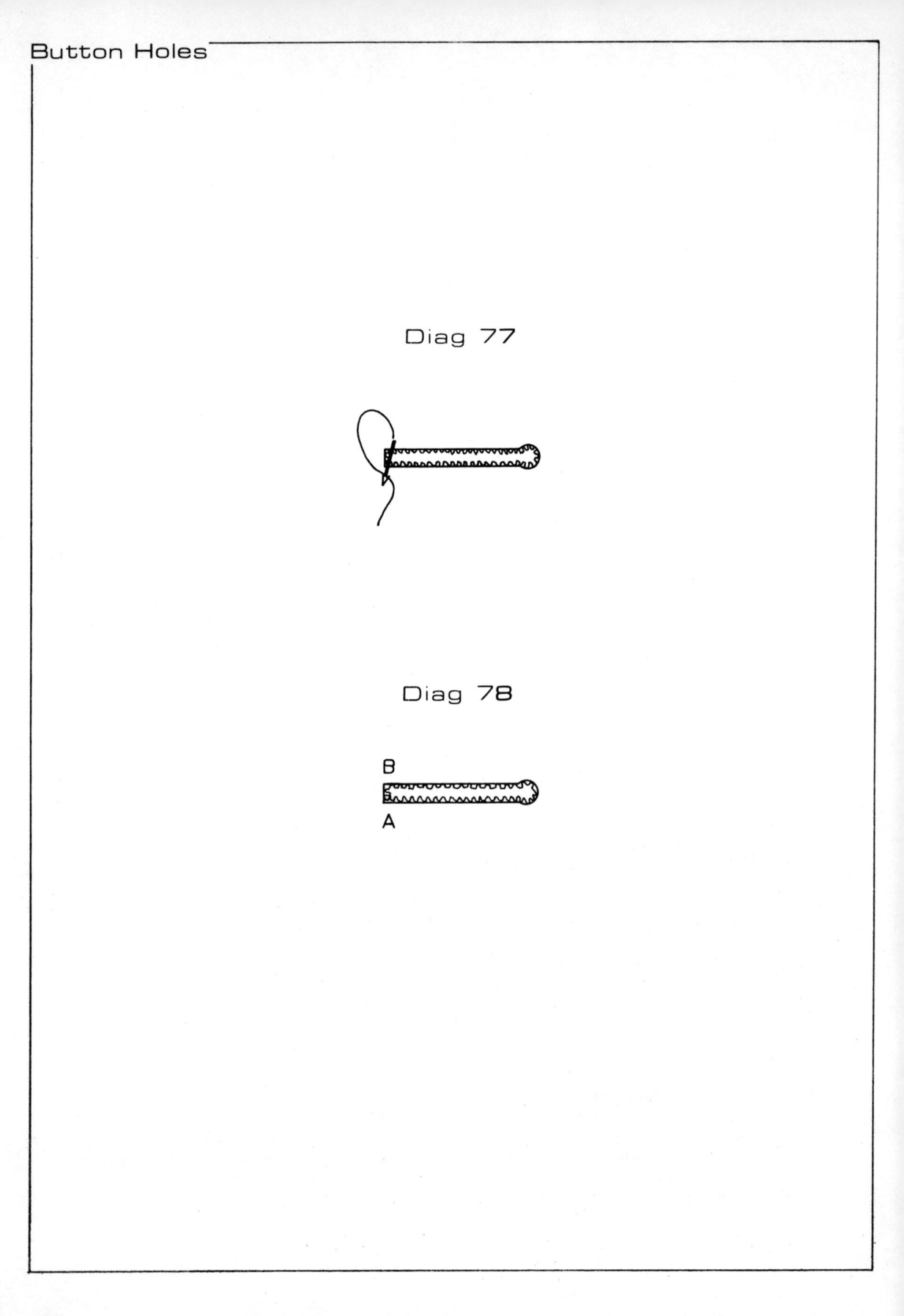

Button Holes

Diag 77

Diag 78

B
A

Twist Button Holes. These are usually made when your garment is finished and almost ready for pressing. There are different thicknesses of twist and you have to decide which one you want to use depending on the weight of your material. Mark your button hole on your garment approximately ¾" away from front edge and cut it open making a slight round at front of hole, use a matching cotton or sylko and over sew all around hole with a blanket stitch. Always start sewing your hole at the back and not the round end. To get a strong button hole place piece of button thread over the edge of the hole which you have oversewn diagram 77 shows button hole stitch. Sew your button hole with a button hole twist using a blanket stitch all around the button hole covering thread and the first layer of chain stitching. When you have sewn all around the button hole you tack the corner from A to B as diagram 78 by stitching over the edge with two or three stitches then push your needle through to the facing side and fasten strongly and cut your twist off at the end. This kind of hole requires a lot of practice and should be tried on a small piece of cloth first. Always remember every stitch should be the same size and as close as possible as this will give an even edge to the hole.

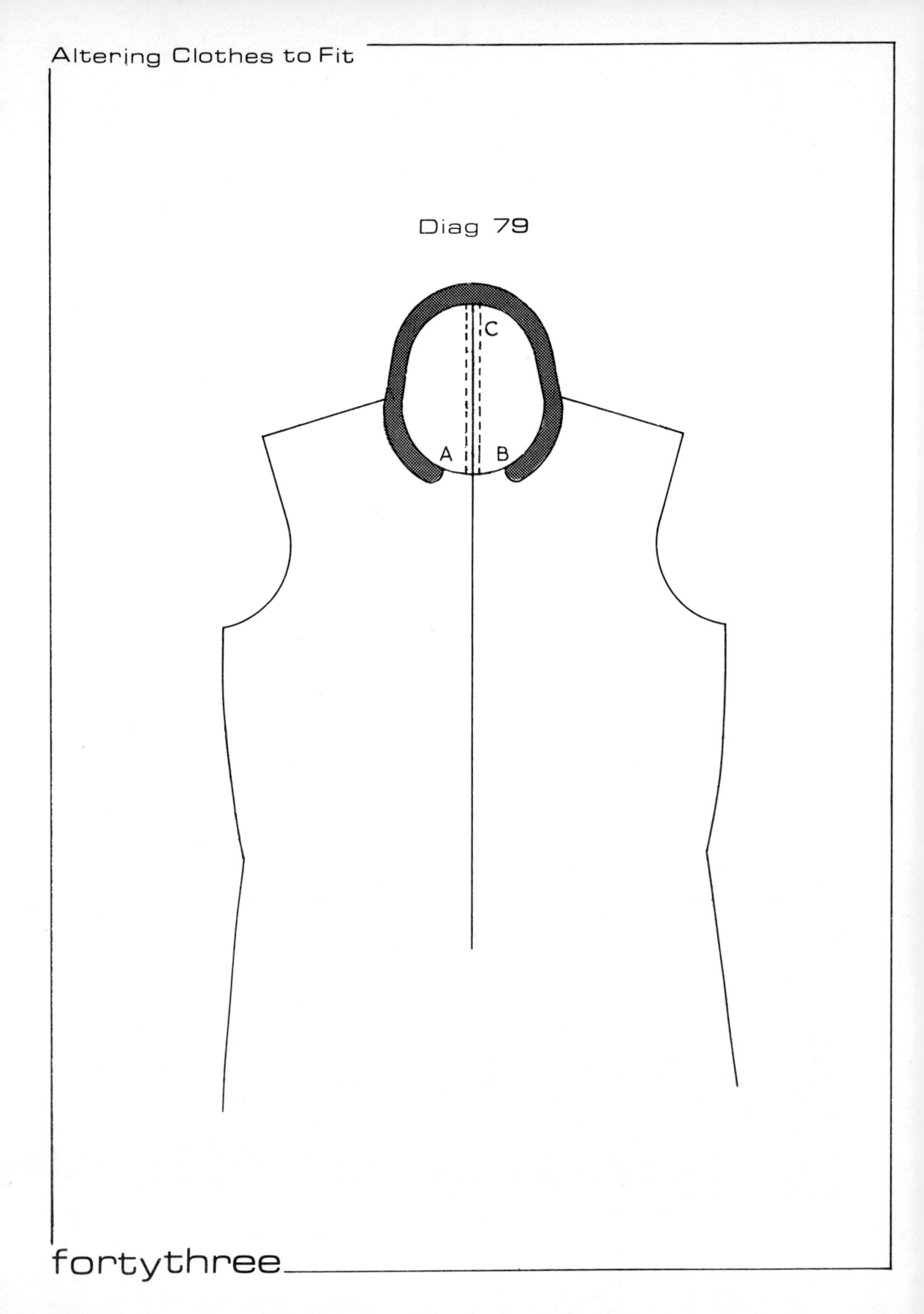

Altering Clothes to Fit

Diag 79

fortythree

Altering Clothes to Fit

Alterations to clothes normally requires a lot of skill and patience. Within the next few pages I will try and help you overcome some of the problems you may have thought were not within your scope. These can be costly when taken to a Tailor or Dressmaker, the answer is do it yourself. You may have lost weight since you bought your favourite dress or coat and find they are now too loose round the neck and slip off your shoulders and are also too big over your bust and hips. The easiest way to overcome this problem is if your garment has a collar you must unpick the collar where it is attached to your garment starting 1" from front at A and finish at 1" from front at B diagram 79. Shaded part in the diagram is the collar which should now be hanging off your garment but being held at the fronts at A and B. C is centre back of garment. Baste a centre back seam at C as broken lines indicate. Usually a seam of about ¾" on the double should be basted to about 9" down by gradually coming into existing seam. If there is no centre seam do not finish 9" down but continue a very narrow seam down to the bottom of dress. This is done when garment fits at waist and hips but is only too big on top. If the garment is too big all through then do not baste centre seam 9" down but continue to baste to bottom of garment taking in ¾" on double all along centre back seam. You next slip on your garment still having collar hanging loose. If you find your garment is still too loose you baste in the centre back making tighter until you get the correct fit. If on the other hand it is too tight you can let out the centre seam to the required size. When you have got the correct fit you sew your centre back seam in the baste. If the garment is lined you adjust the lining in the same way making the same alteration. You next rebaste your collar on to your garment. This should be basted ⅝" lower at centre back of garment and ⅜" lower at shoulder seams to present position at A and B diagram 79. A, B and C on diagram 80 indicates old neck line whilst D, E and F is the new neck line where collar should now be basted.

Once collar has been basted to neck fit your garment on once again and make certain that the collar and shoulders are now fitting correctly otherwise if not the collar can be raised slightly or lowered to get the correct balance. Once this is done you can finish the alteration. You will be surprised how good you will feel after having completed a major task.

Altering Clothes to Fit

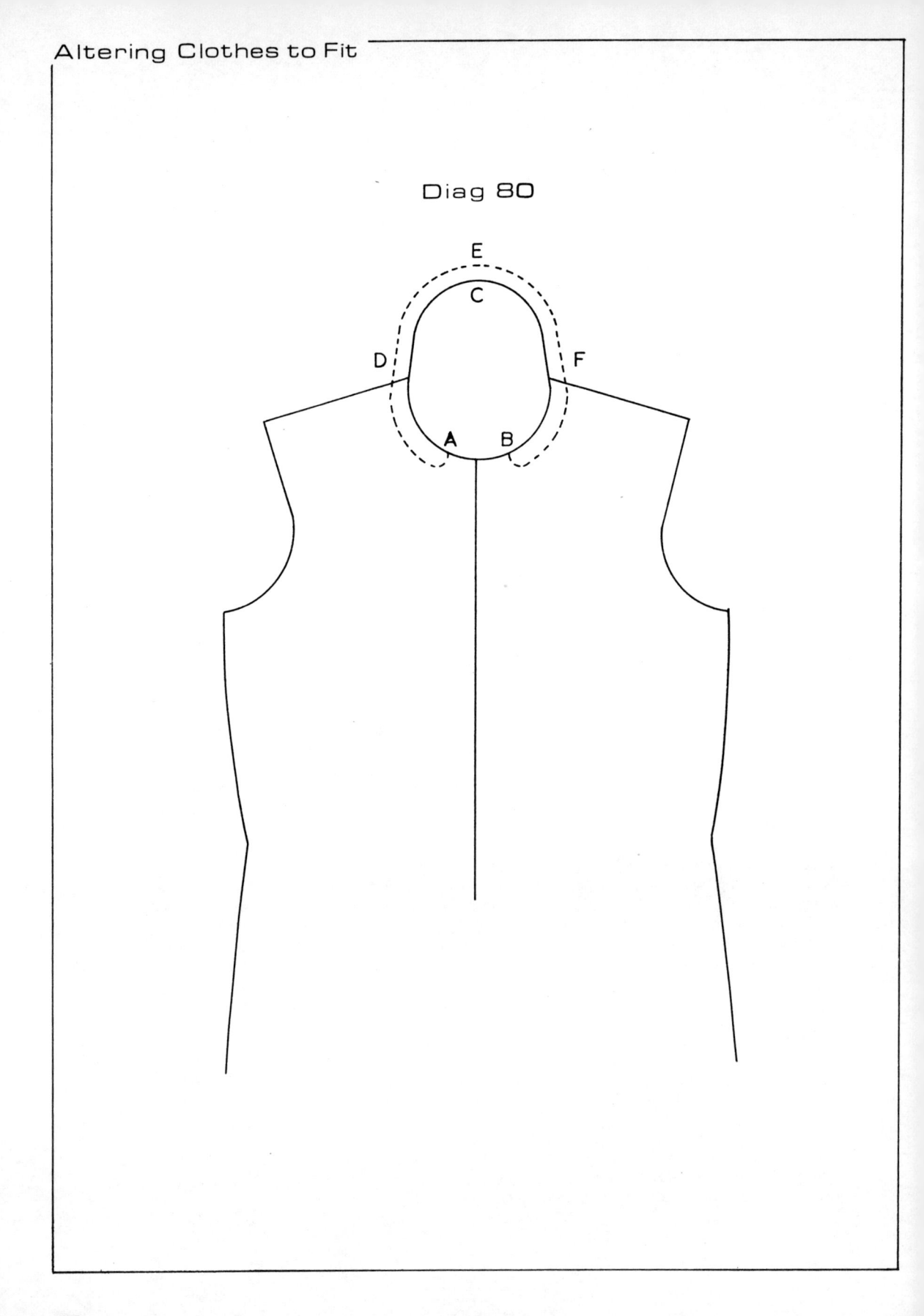

Diag 80

Letting out Waists and Seats of Slax

This is usually done through the centre back seam. If there is a waist band or lining or petersham band this must be unpicked at centre back seam, approximately 2" each side of back seam. You then unpick centre back seam and providing there is inlay allowed you let out the required amount at the waist down to seat of slax.

If there is no material to let out you may find that at the bottom of your trouser legs there is enough material turned back which can be cut out and used. This should be cut into a V shape using the wider part for the top. Failing this one must try to match a material as near as possible to use. You then set a piece of material into your waist, press open seams and resew waist band back on to slax.

By altering them this way you will not spoil the line of your slax and the centre front will not be put out of place.

Letting out Waists and Hips of Skirts

This can be done by letting out required amount wherever inlays have been allowed. Firstly your waist must be unpicked away from skirt where inlays are going to be let out. Once you have unpicked your seams and let them out and resewn them, press open seams. Your waistband will now be too tight to replace. To extend you cut through waistband and set in a piece of cloth the same amount as you have let out at your waist. This material can be taken from the hem of your skirt. You then resew waist band onto skirt.

If there are no inlays to let out and the skirt has back darts these can be unpicked and let out. This may give you an extra 2" to 3" on your waist. Sometimes by only letting out your back darts you will find that is all you need do apart from setting in a piece of material into your waistband, this being the same quantity as you have let out on your skirt.

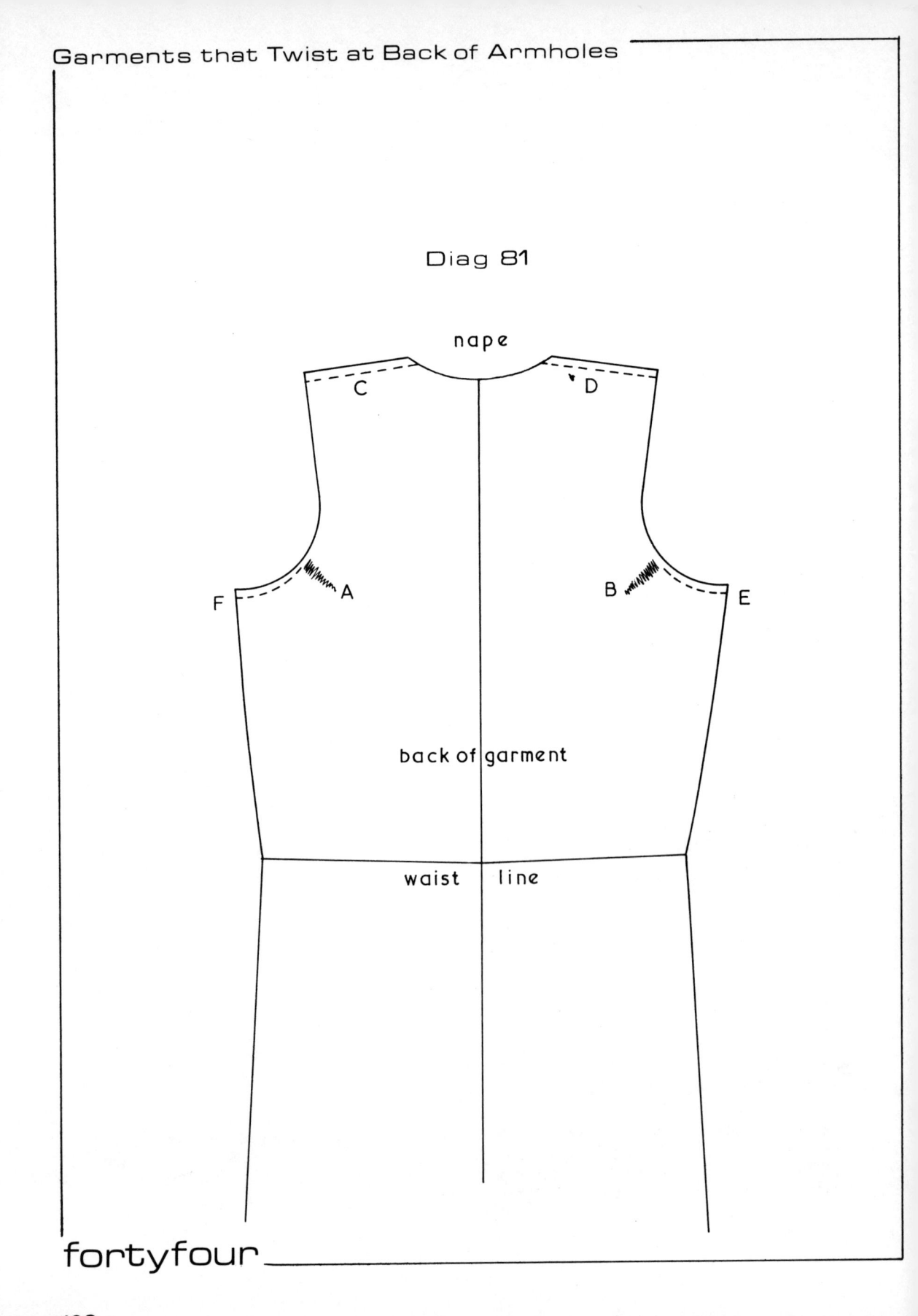

Garments that Twist at Back of Armholes

Diag 81

nape

C　　D

F　A　　B　E

back of garment

waist line

fortyfour

Garments that Twist at Back of Arm Holes

This is quite a common occurrence due to the fact that your garment is cut too long from nape of neck to your waist line.

Diagram 81 shows A and B where the garment often twists. To overcome this take your own measurement from nape of neck down to waist line. Then measure your garment from nape to waist line the difference between the two measurements is the cause of the trouble. You now reduce your shoulder line C and D the excess amount above your natural measurement from nape to waist line. Rebaste your shoulder seams and fit on garment before sewing shoulder seams as you may now find the armholes are too tight, if this is so, you should lower your armholes as shown on diagram 81 at E and F. This alteration will completely clear up the trouble.

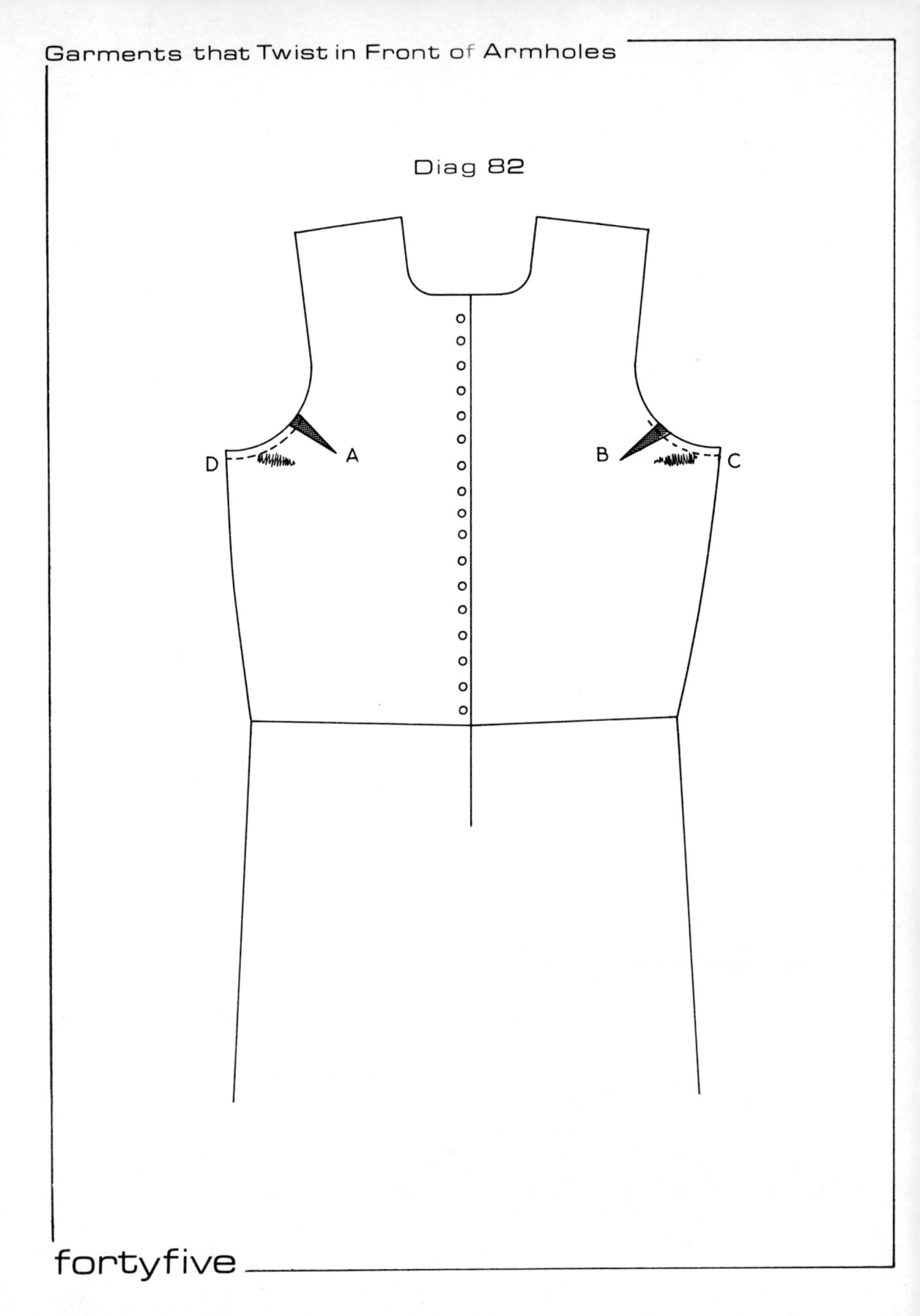

Garments that Twist in Front of Armholes

Diag 82

fortyfive

Garments that Twist in Front of Arm Holes

This alteration is done differently to the twist at the back of armholes. The easiest way to do this is to baste a ¾" dart as shown on diagram 82 at A and B. Wavy lines indicate twist in garment. Before sewing dart fit on your garment as you may find ¾" dart is not deep enough to clear the twist. If this is so you should baste a deeper dart until the twist has completely disappeared. It may be necessary to lower armholes at C and D diagram 82 the amount can be judged when fitting on garment.

Clothes that are too Tight

Diag 83

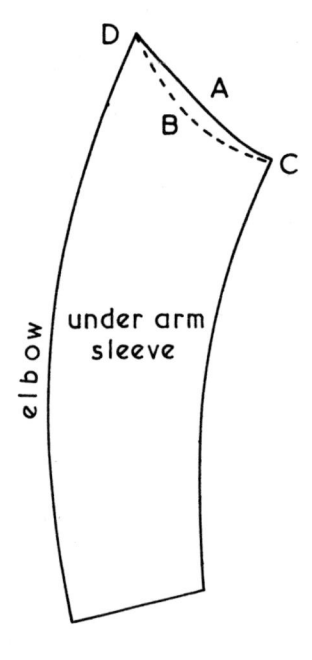

D
A
B
C

elbow   under arm
        sleeve

fortysix

Clothes that are too tight

If you have a coat or dress that is uncomfortable when putting your arms forward or unable to raise your arms with ease, your remedy lies either in easing centre back or underarms.

If there are inlays in the centre back start from nothing at top nape of neck and gradually let out seam at scye line as this is where it is needed most to give you the extra width across your back when bringing your arms forward. From your scye line gradually start running your seam back to your waist line centre back seam. If there is no cloth to let out at back, your next step is to see if there is any material to let out at top of side seams under the arms. Unpick armhole 2" each side of side seams and let out required amount down to waist. You will now find that the sleeve will be too tight to replace. To overcome this you hollow out your sleeves as shown in diagram 83 A is natural line of sleeve. Broken line at B is hollowed section. This should be hollowed out ½" at A to nothing at C and D. If you still find the sleeves too tight to replace in armhole you can stretch your under sleeve from C to D by using a hot steam iron and slightly wet the sleeve where you will be stretching the material at B. If it is a lined garment you must alter the lining doing the same alteration as you do to your garment. You should now be able to reset your sleeve and finish the alteration. This will give you a comfortably fitted garment.

If there are no inlays to let out either at centre back or underarm side seams the only thing left to do is unpick the armhole 1" to the back of side seam to 3½" in front, which should be in the same position as B diagram 83. Hollow out sleeve at B ½" and hollow out same amount of your armhole on garment.

Replace sleeve and finish off.

This will give an added amount of ease and comfort to you.

How to make a Skirt from your Slax without using a Pattern

Diag 84.

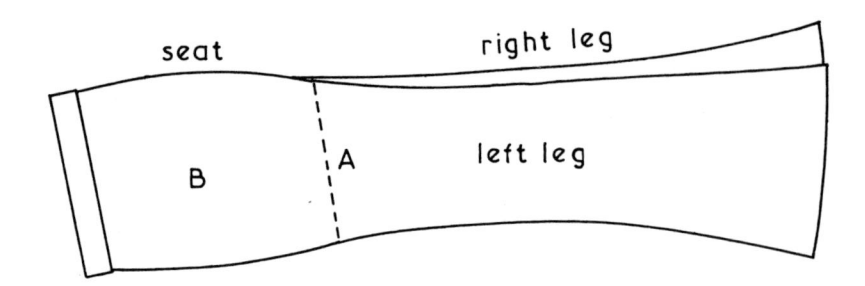

seat — right leg — left leg — B — A

Diag 85

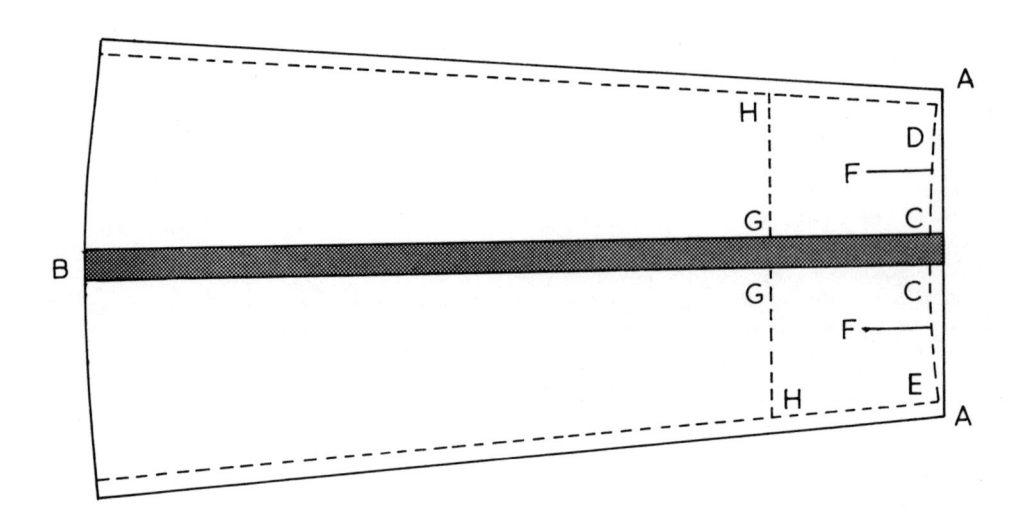

A — H — D — F — G — C — B — G — C — F — H — E — A

fortyseven

How to make a Skirt from your Slax without using a pattern

Your old or unwanted slax should not be thrown away as you can make a smart skirt for yourself or for a child. By using the leg section you can make a fitted four gore or inverted pleated skirt.

Firstly you cut off the legs at top at A broken lines diagram 84 shows. Unpick both inside leg seams and bottom hem. Do not unpick outside leg seam. Press the bottoms.

Lay both pieces of cloth on top of each other wrong side out as diagram 85. A is the bottom part of trousers which will now be the waist line of skirt, whilst B will be the bottom. C is the outside leg seam of your slax. Broken line at C is ½" down at centre seam. D and E from C are both ¼" of your waist measurement plus ½" to allow for back darts at F. No front darts are included. Should they be required add another ½" each side of waist measurement. G is 7" down from C. H is measured from G which is ¼" hip measurement. Broken line is sewing line. B from A is required length of skirt. Run side seams down to bottom from H but through broken line from A through C along to A. Now baste stitch through broken lines which are side seams and darts. Baste zip in top of left side seam and turn up hem at bottom. You now have a four gored skirt ready for fitting.

To make a knife or inverted pleat in skirt use top section of your slax diagram 84 section B. Cut strip 4" to 6" wide and insert cloth in front seam at G diagram 85. If back pleat is required you insert a similar piece of material as for front pleat. You then press your pleats to knife or inverted. After fitting your skirt and making any adjustments you may find necessary you finish your skirt in the usual way.

Making a Sleeve Length Poncho without using a Pattern

Diag 86

centre of cloth

B A C
D

selvedge selvedge

Diag 87

I
B C
H

fortyeight

Making a Sleeve Length Poncho without using a pattern

This is one of the easy things to make and requires very little skill.

For this you require 1¾ yards material approximately 60" wide.

Open out your material and fold in half across width of material as diagram 86 shows. A is centre of material. B and C are both 2¾" from A. Mark a semi-circle from A to B around to D and C. Mark out a semi-circle by placing your tape measure at A and extend to E which is full distance of material and mark out through F to G.

Now open out your material and you should have a circle as diagram 87. Cut from C to B around D and back to C. Cut down from D to H which is 7". This is the opening for the front of your poncho. Cut around broken line from C to B just slightly rounding to 1 approximately ⅜".

You now bind your edges bottom and neck. This can be done by using the pieces of material saved from the sides of your circle, but be certain to cut the material on the bias and join up into a long strip approximately 1" wide.

Relining Skirt without a Pattern

Diag 88

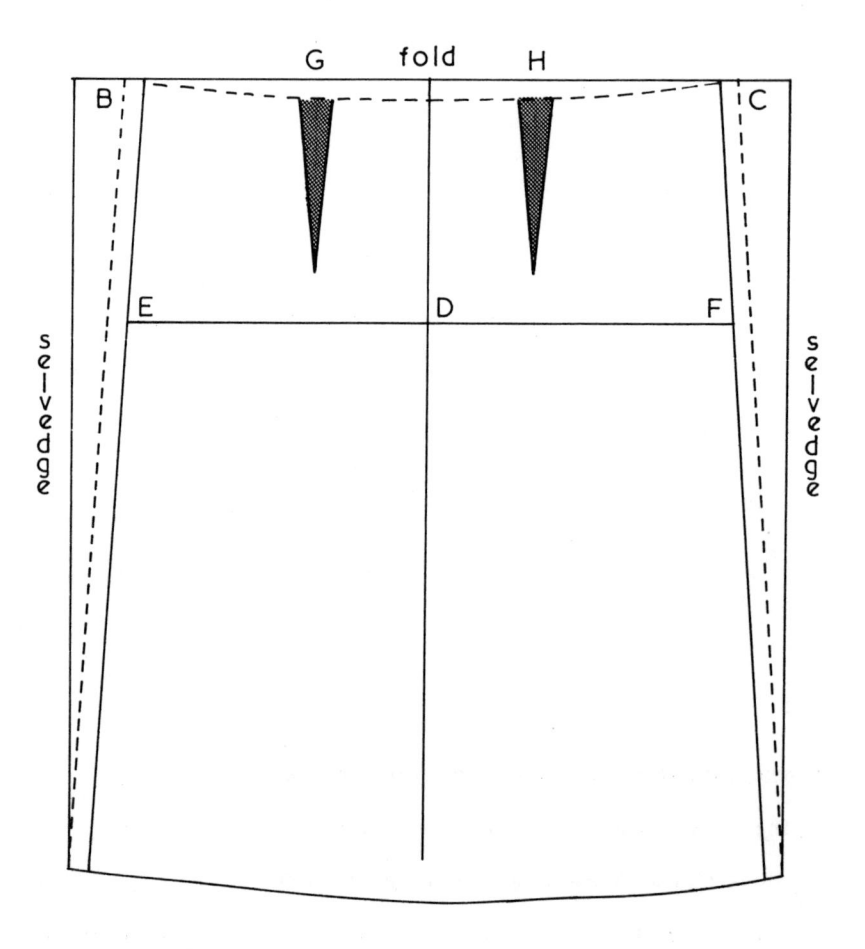

fortynine

Relining Skirt without a pattern

The most simple way to get your lining to fit correctly is to be sure it is cut to the correct size. The quantity of lining you will require depends on the width of the bottom of your skirt. If the lining you use is wider than this you only need one length, but should the lining be narrower then two lengths of lining are required — one for the front and one for the back. When using the narrow lining you fold over your lining as diagram 88 shows with selvedge at the sides but if using the wider lining the fold should be at one side and selvedge at the other either right or left side of you.

A is centre of lining, measure your skirt waist and add 1" plus 1" for every dart you have in your skirt.

B and C are both ¼ of this measurement coming from A.

D is 7½" down from A.

E and F are both a ¼ of your hip measurement extending from D. For example if your hips measurement is 40" then E and F should both be 10" from D.

Chalk your side seam starting at top B and C through E and F down to bottom which should be the width of your skirt.

Mark your darts in the linings the same position as they appear in your skirt as shown by shaded section on diagram 88 at G and H.

You cut your lining allowing 1" inlay at side seams and sew your seams in the chalk marks leaving an opening on top of your left side seam 7½" long this will allow for your zip opening.

Turn up hem at bottom and press your lining which should now be ready for sewing into skirt all around waist and zip opening.

Fly Front for Slax

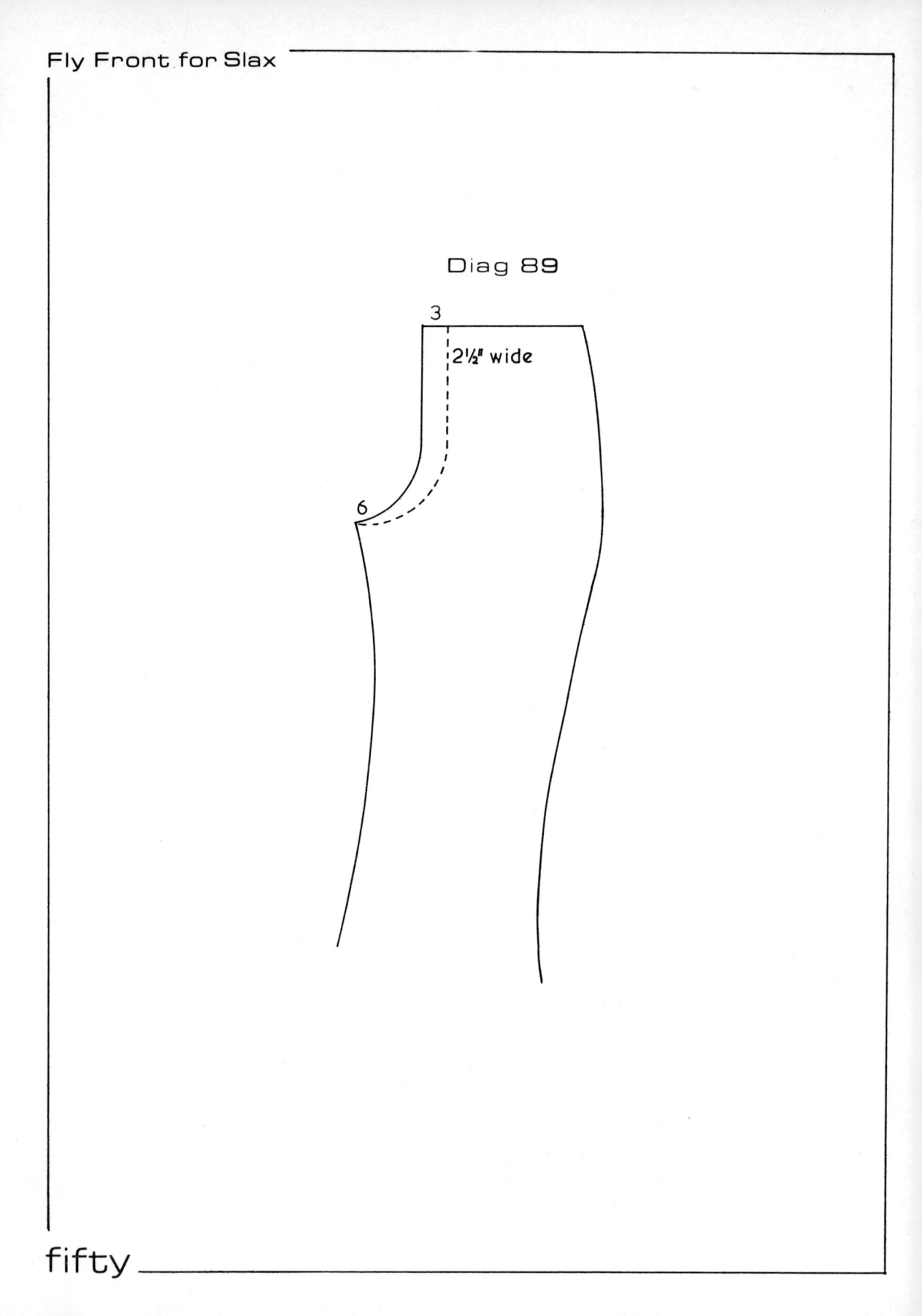

Diag 89

3

2½" wide

6

fifty

Fly Fronts for Slax

To make a fly front you cut two pieces of material which have to fit at fronts of slax from 3 to 6 diagram 89. To do this lay out front section of slax on to cloth and chalk on cloth from 3 to 6. Now remove slax fronts and cut your material 2½" wide on top to nothing at 6 as diagram 89

shows (broken lines). Sew fly pieces on, one on each section from 3 to 6. Take left leg section and turn back fly and stitch down all around ⅜" away from inside edge which is ⅜" nearer to the front of broken line on dia. 89 and make certain that the front seam from 3 to 6 does not show over the front edge. If you baste edge from 3 to 6 and press before stitching this would prevent edge seam from showing.

Press open seam from 3 to 6 right leg section. You can face this section of fly right leg with lining to give a clean finish. Now make up your slax and sew in your zip.

Trouser Side Pockets

Diag 90

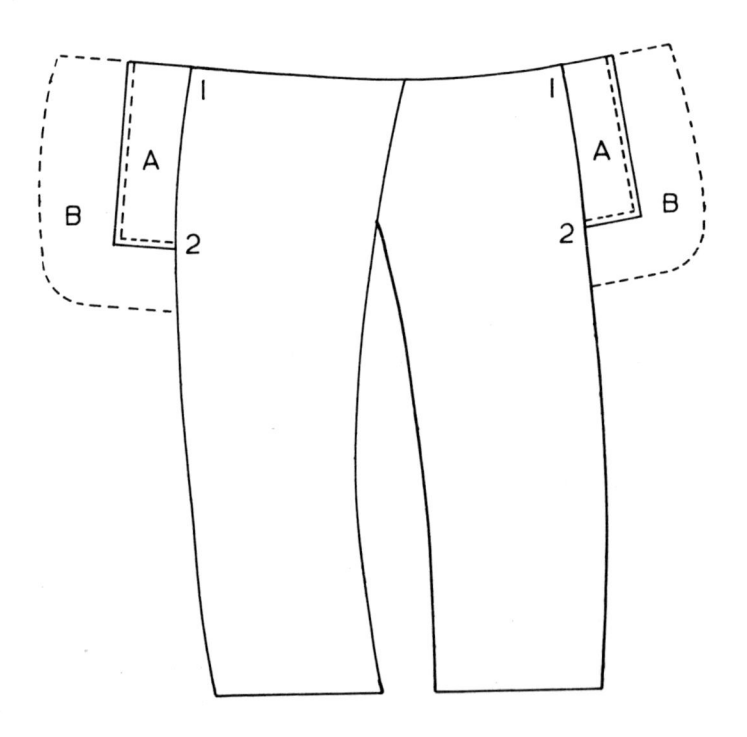

fiftyone

Trouser Side Pockets

Before making your pockets, sew up seat seam and inside leg seam, **not** outside leg seam. Fly seam or zip fly should now be sewn.

You require two pieces of your trouser material for each pocket, each to be approximately 2½" by 2" longer than the required finished size. Sew them on one each side of slax from 1 towards 2 as diagram 90 shows on both front and back sections of trousers. The outside of your trousers should be facing you. Cut your pocket linings as broken lines indicate about 6" wide and 3" longer than pocket facing from 1 to 2. Take one piece of lining and place under each facing sections A and machine on all around sections A turning in raw edge of cloth at B. You now take the fronts of your slax and fold back sections A from 1 to 2 to the inside of your slax and stitch down the edge as diagram 91 broken line at C ¼" away from edge.

Take the back of your slax and press open seam from 1 to 2 diagram 90. Place your front and back sections of slax on top of each other with the outside of slax facing you. You should now have your pocket linings facing you. Machine all around your pocket linings and your pockets are now complete. You now machine your outside leg seam and finish off your slax. Both male or female slax are made in the same way when making side pockets.

Trouser Side Pockets

Diag 91

Diag 91 (continued below)

Fronts   Back

Using an old pattern for a changed figure

You may have a dress pattern that did fit you in the past but have outgrown it in some places, or you may have lost weight and now find that to cut a garment using the same pattern would result in having something that does not fit correctly; or you may like the style of the pattern and would like to use it to make something for a relative or friend.

By using the following instructions you will avoid having to cut or even buy a new pattern.

You start by taking your correct measurements as diagram 1 and instructions on Pages 10 and 11.

Lay your back pattern onto your material and mark it out in the usual way, **but do not cut.** You now take away your pattern and mark your adjustments according to your measurements as follows:

First check your cross back measurement to see if any alteration is required.

Broken lines on diagram 92 shows where adjustments are made — either bigger or smaller — for example if cross back is to be ½" bigger than the pattern you allow ¼" each side at 1, or if it is to be ½" smaller you reduce ¼" each side running up to shoulder, shoulder width can be adjusted to any width you choose as broken lines indicate.

Bust measurement should now be checked, if size is to be increased, extend a quarter of the extra amount at side seam at 2 coming out to broken line at 3 and running into broken line cross back at 1. If size is to be reduced you come in from 2 to 4 a quarter of the amount; for example if pattern is 2" too big you come in ½" from 2 to 4 and run line into new cross back line. Shoulder line should now be adjusted accordingly by ¼" either way from 5 to 6, raised for larger size and lowered for smaller size and adjust accordingly from 5 to 7.

Waist or hip lines may require raising or lowering to your new measurements. This should be marked out on your material, measure being taken from back neck at 7 diagram 92 down to your waist and then down to your hip line. You can now increase or decrease your waist and hip measurements to any size you require. Always remember you either add or reduce a quarter of the amount required on each seam at waist or hips in the same way as you have done at the bust line.

You may find that the waist or hip measurement required is still the same size as your pattern, or either one of them only wants altering. In these circumstances you only alter where necessary, and continue your side seam by running your seam into existing seam.

The front of your dress now has to be altered. You do the same alteration as you have done to the back of your dress. The amount you have altered at your cross back, scye line, waist, hips and shoulders should be repeated on your front. 8 at front of shoulders diagram 92 should be adjusted the same amount as from 5 to 7 of back neck.

Altering the sleeves to fit the armhole:

10 from 9 is the same distance as 3 from 2.

11 from 9 is same as 4 from 2.

13 and 14 are both ¼" from 12, 13 for the larger sleeve and 14 for smaller sleeve.

Run line for new size sleeve on your material from 13 to 10 to nothing at cuff or from 14 to 11 to nothing at cuff.

Should you want to make a wider cuff you can continue the extra width all down from 10 to the bottom of sleeve.

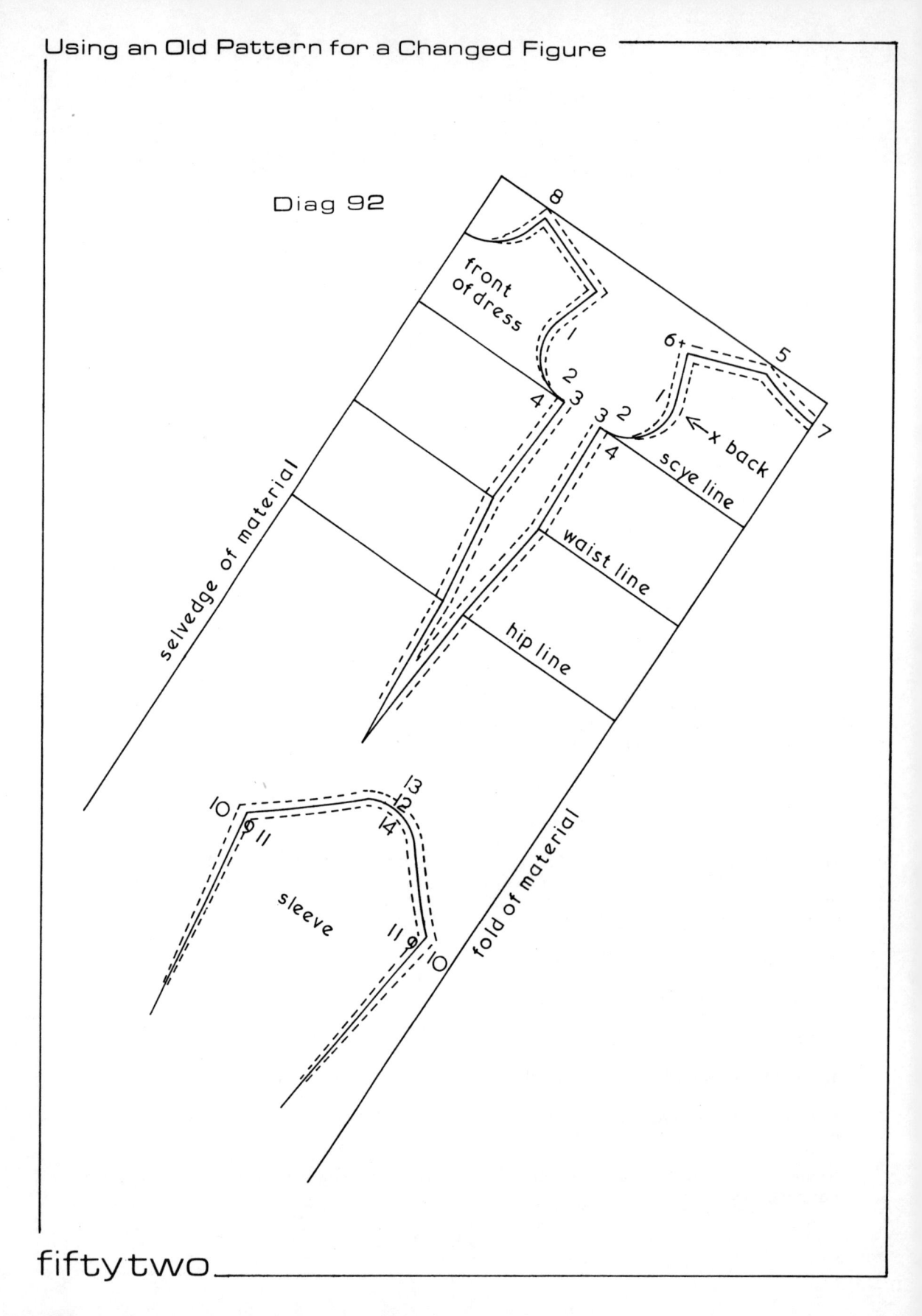

Using an Old Pattern for a Changed Figure

Diag 92

front of dress

scye line

x back

waist line

hip line

selvedge of material

fold of material

sleeve

fifty two

138

Using an old pattern for a changed figure (continued)

Cutting a blouse or skirt from an old pattern is done in the same way. When cutting a skirt from an old pattern be certain to have your hip line measurement the correct distance down from your waist line before making any adjustments. Once this is done you can cut your skirt as long or as short as you wish to wear it. If you are making a pleated skirt you can raise or lower your pleats accordingly.

Cutting a Waistcoat and Skirt without a Paper Pattern

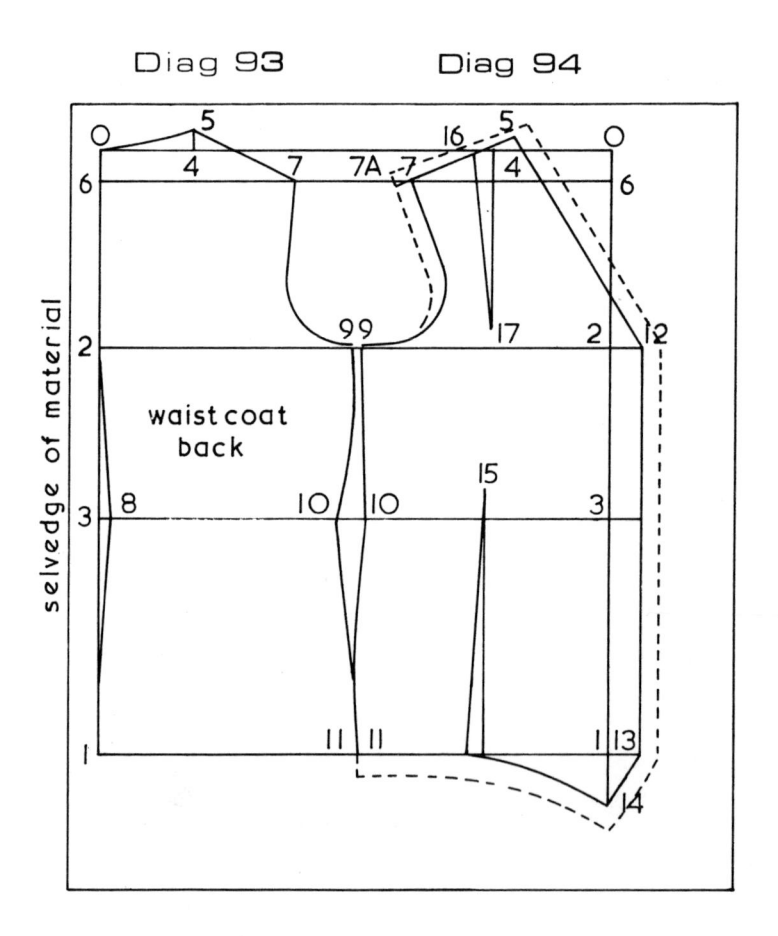

Diag 93   Diag 94

waist coat back

fiftythree

Cutting a Waistcoat and Skirt without a paper pattern

For those of my readers who feel confident enough to cut without a pattern, I have written the instructions to guide you on your way.

Diagram 93 is marked out directly on to your material. Quantity required is your length of back from 0 to 1 plus 4". This is for a cloth with a minimum width of 54", or twice your length from 0 to 1 plus 8" for a 36" width material. If using a 36" width material this should be opened out and folded in halves so that the selvedge edge is at 0 to 1 which is your centre back and fold of material is at top diagram 93 and 94.

1 from 0 is your required back length plus ½" for seams.

2 from 0 is ¼ of your bust measurement.

3 from 0 is your natural waist line down from 0. Square out lines on your material from 0 – 1 – 2 and 3.

4 is one twelfth of bust measurement plus ⅜" coming out from 0.

For example if your bust measurement is 36" then 4 from 0 is 3 ⅜", if your bust is 42" then 4 from 0 would be 3 ⅞".

5 is always ¾" up from 4.

6 is 1½" from 0.

7 from 6 is 1" less than half the cross back measure.

8 is ½" from 3.

Shape centre back from 0 to 8 down to 1.

9 is ¼ bust measurement plus ¾" to allow for centre back and side seams.

10 is shaped in a ½" coming down from 9.

11 from 1 is ½" wider than 9 from 2.

Now shape armhole and side seam from 7 to 9 and down to 11 as diagram 93 shows.

Your back should now be cut out and centre back should be cut out straight from 0 to 1, do not yet shape out at 8 until fronts of waistcoat are marked out. Now place your back onto remainder of the material as diagram 94 and mark out all around your back. This will give you two back sections. Do not cut yet as this has to be remarked for your fronts. Before doing this you now take away your back and shape it at 8 on your centre back.

We now proceed to mark out the front section:

12 is 1" from 2, this is squared down to 13.

Run line from 5 to 12.

14 is extended approximately 2½" to 3" from 1, this depends on your own personal taste.

Shape bottom of garment from 13 down to 14 and on to 11.

15 is front dart which is left to your own discretion.

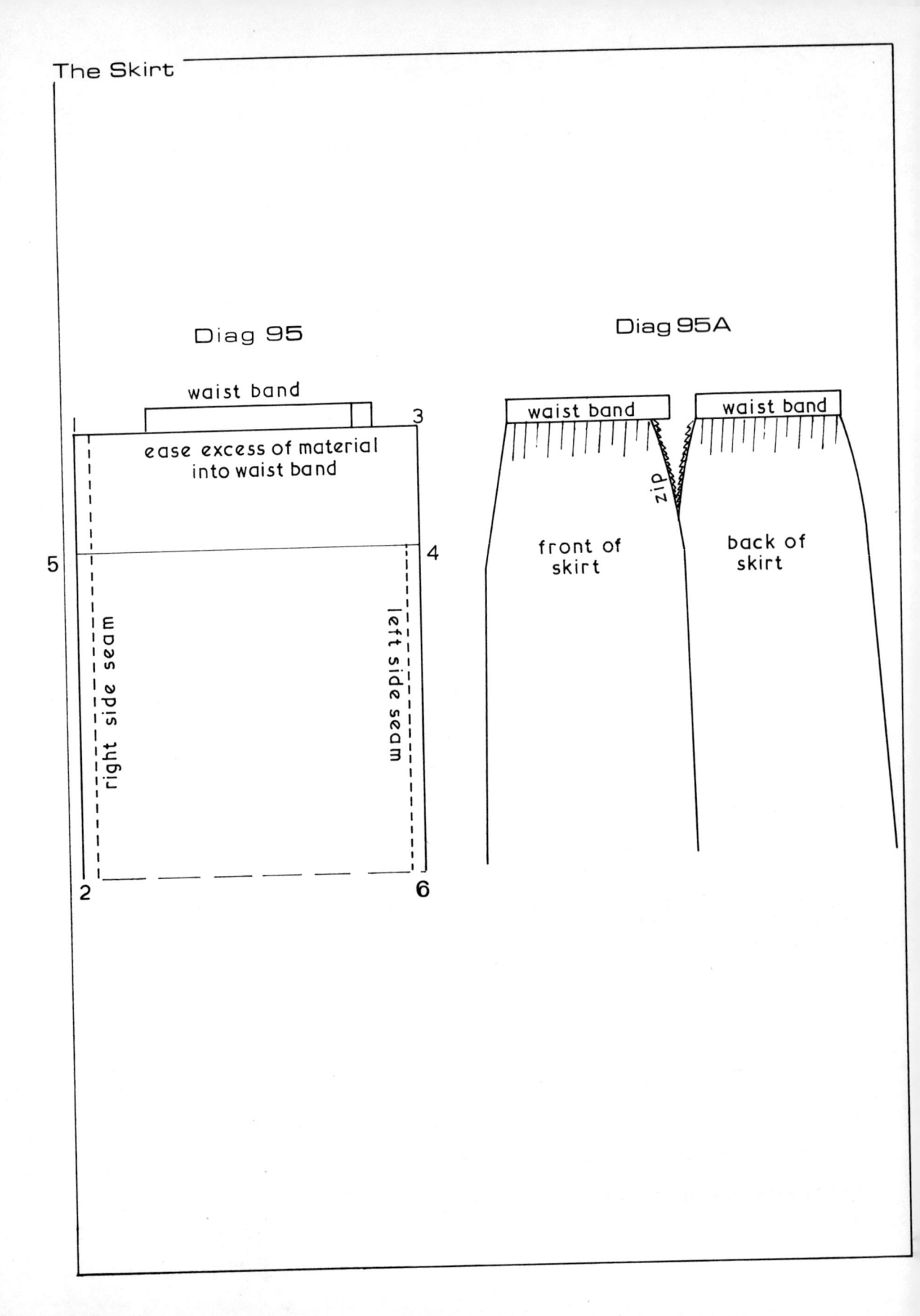

The Skirt

Diag 95

waist band

ease excess of material into waist band

right side seam

left side seam

2, 3, 4, 5, 6

Diag 95A

waist band   waist band

zip

front of skirt   back of skirt

Cutting a Waistcoat and Skirt without a paper pattern (continued)

Broken lines are approximately 1½" allowances for facings.

For a prominently busted person shoulder darts should be cut.

For this you extend shoulder at 7 to 7a 2½". Broken lines are new shoulder and armhole line.

Mark out a 2" dart as shown at 16 and 17, 16 being 1½" from 5 and 17 is 1½" up from bust line.

Your fronts are now ready for cutting, this completes the cutting of your waistcoat.

If garment is to be lined cut lining the same size as the waistcoat.

Pockets look rather nice in a waistcoat but this I leave to your own discretion refer to pocket section of book. When finished button holes should be made always on right hand side of fronts for a ladies garment.

The Skirt

This is a pencil line skirt eased in around the waist and very easy to cut and make. If you are using a 54" material or wider, you will require your full length plus 3" for waist seam and hem. If you are using a 36" wide material you will require double the quantity.

You start by cutting a 3" strip off the width of your material for your waistband. This should be cut 1½" longer than your natural waist measurement; if your waist measures say, 28" you will require this to measure 29½" x 3" wide.

Diagram 95 shows a double layer of material on your cutting board or table.

Mark a line going down from 1 to 2 for your length plus ½" extra for seam allowance on the waist line. The balance at the bottom is to be left on for your hem.

3 from 1 is half your hip measurement plus 1" for seams.

4 is 7½" down from 3.

5 from 4 is the same measurement as 3 from 1.

6 from 3 is the same measurement as 2 from 1.

Broken line from 3 to 4 is 1½" out for sewing zip onto.

You now cut around your chalk lines leaving on bottom hem. Machine side seams of skirt, right side to be sewn the full length of your material from 1 to 2. Left side to be sewn from 4 to bottom at 6. Broken lines on diagram 95 indicate machine stitching. 3 to 4 is left open for zip.

The ends of the waistband should now be sewn up. Baste waistband onto skirt, easing skirt into the waistband all around leaving 1" of waistband to extend over front of left side seam as diagram 95A shows, shaded part is band extension. Zip can now be sewn in, and fastener should be sewn on extension of wasitband.

Baste up the bottom of the skirt and fit for length before finishing.

This will give you a smart outfit and can be worn with a blouse or the waistcoat can be worn with separate slacks or contrasting skirt.

Cutting Checked or Striped Materials

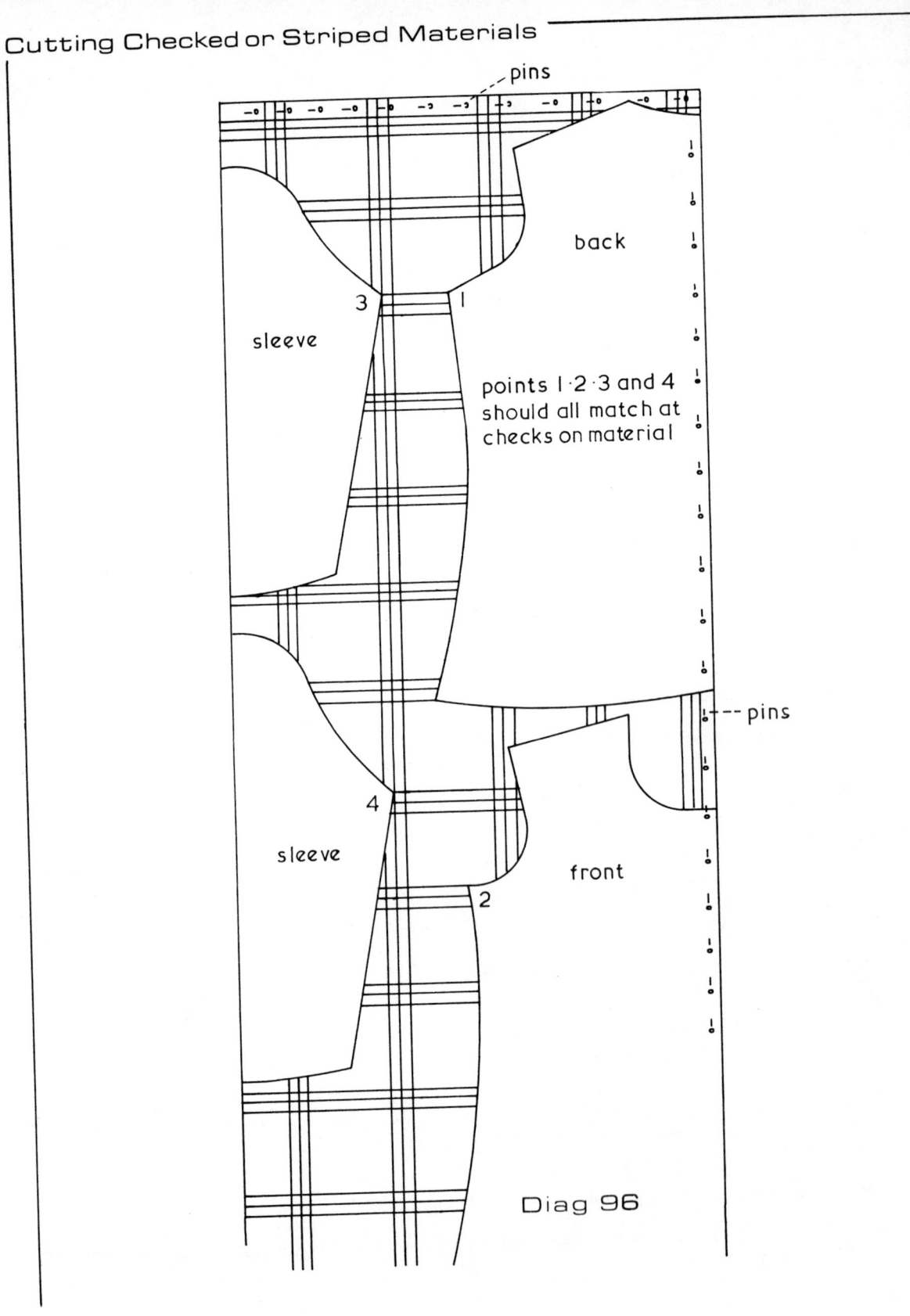

pins

back

sleeve

3 1

points 1·2·3 and 4 should all match at checks on material

pins

sleeve

4

2

front

Diag 96

fifty four

Cutting Checked or Striped Materials

When cutting it is very important that stripes or checks should match. Therefore, for a check material always buy ¼ yard more material than you normally would for the garment you are making. When working on a double width material the first thing to do is to pin your cloth together at top and selvedge edge with stripes or checks matching.

For striped material you can now proceed to cut knowing that the stripes going down will be correct.

When using a check material you must be sure to get your side seams and sleeves to match.

First lay either your front or back pattern onto your material, the top and bottom of side seams should both be in the same position on the check, as diagram 96.

Place your sleeve pattern onto your material with the top of your under arm seam being in the same position as the top of side seam is from check as diagram 96.

This will give you a garment with side seams and sleeves all matching.

When cutting a skirt or any other article of clothing using a check material, always cut in the same way so that wherever two sections are to be sewn together be sure that the top and bottom of each section are cut the same distance from check.

Cutting and Making a Tiered Skirt without a Pattern

One and two tiered skirts

Diag 97

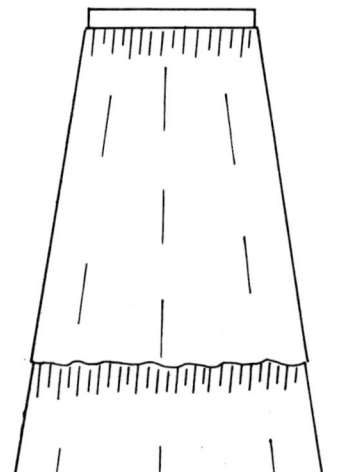

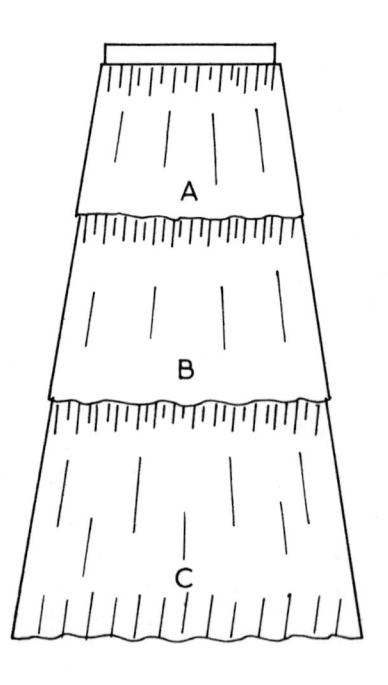

Diag 98 — A, B, C

fiftyfive

Cutting and Making a Tiered Skirt Without a Pattern

Tiered skirts are easy to cut and make, and for one who is handy with the needle, exciting and pleasing results will be achieved.

Firstly there are only two measurements required, the waist and the length. In this instance we will work on a 28" waist and a 31" length.

Diagrams 97 and 98 are one and two tiered skirts. It is preferable to use a 60" wide material to avoid joins. If using a narrower material tiers can be cut lengthwise to avoid joining. You require two pieces of material for the top of the skirt — one for the front and one for the back sections as diagram 98 section A, each to be approximately 9" wider than half your waist measurement. As we are working on a 28" waist this should be 14" plus 9" which equals 23" wide, and to be cut 8¾" long, this includes seam allowances for the top and the bottom as broken lines on daigram 99 indicate.

Section B on diagram 99 is the first tier. For this you require two pieces of material, each to be 12¾" long, this includes seam allowances, and should be 21" wider than half the waist measurement, which equals 35".

Section C on diagram 99 is for the second tier. For this you require two pieces of material both measuring 11¾" long, this includes seam and 1" hem allowance, and to be 38" wider than waist measurement, this equals 52" wide.

Cut waistband to your waist measurement size plus 2", this is for seams and overlap for sewing on fasteners and should be cut 2¾" wide, this will give a 1" wide band when sewn on turned back and finished.

You should now be able to cut this skirt to any required size by following these instructions and decreasing or increasing the waist and length to any desired size.

To increase or decrease fullness of tiers you simply add or subtract the width allowances plus half the waist measurement.

You now proceed to sew. First take section A and sew up right side seam, then the left side seam, this seam sew ¾" up from bottom taking a 1¼" seam, the top part is left open to baste zip into.

You now sew side seams in sections B and C. Pin sections 1 and 2 together and 3 and 4 together and ease in section B all around evenly into section A. Sections 5, 6, 7 and 8 are joined together in the same way.

Baste zip into opening at the top of the left side seam and sew your waist band on top of section A easing section A all around waistband. Baste 1" hem at bottom and fit on skirt before finishing to be certain that the waist and length measurements are correct.

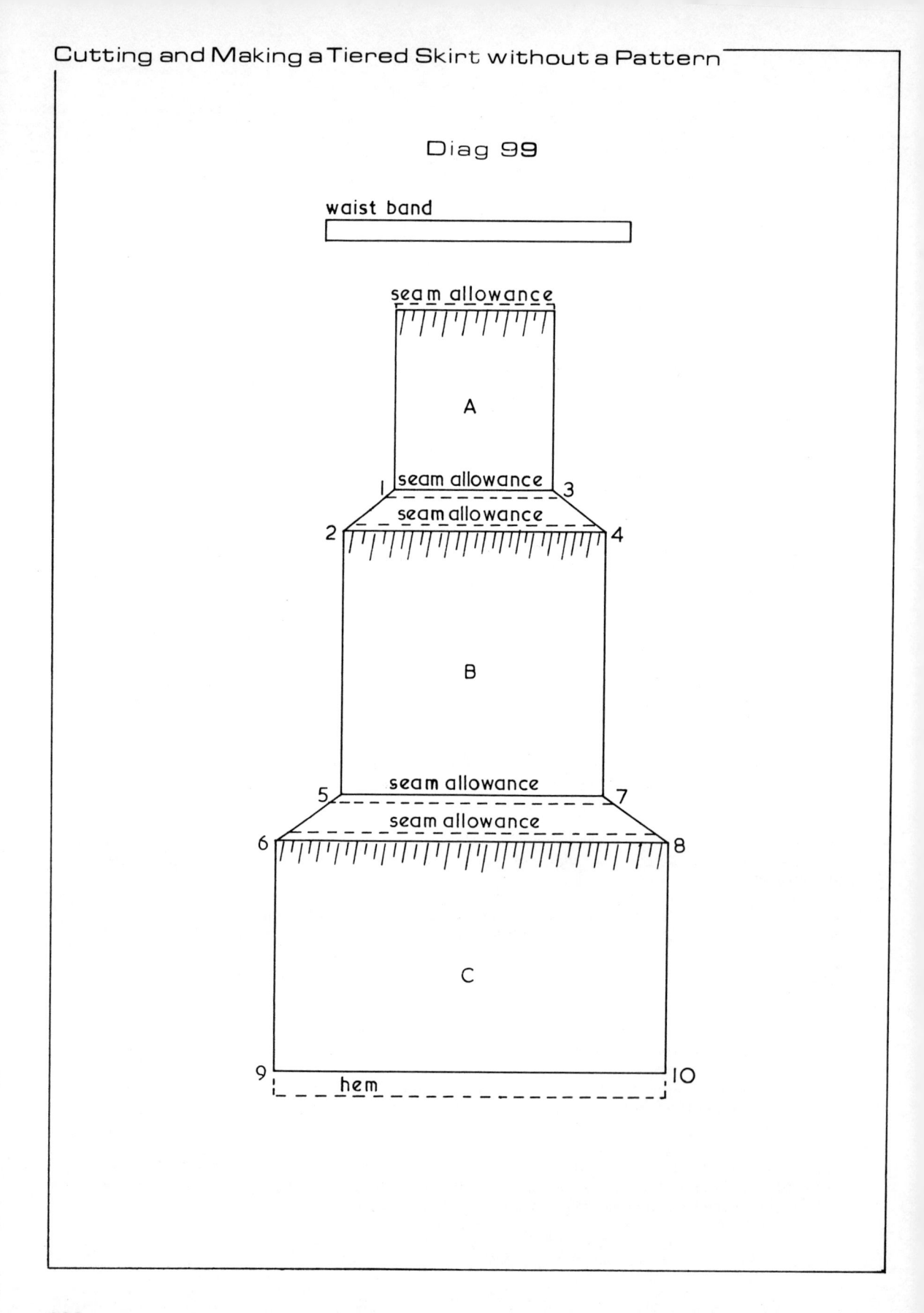

Cutting and Making a Tiered Skirt without a Pattern

Diag 99

waist band

seam allowance

A

1 seam allowance 3
2 seam allowance 4

B

5 seam allowance 7
6 seam allowance 8

C

9 hem 10

Cutting and Making a Tiered Skirt without a pattern (continued)

The One Tier Skirt. When cutting a one tier skirt the principle is the same except that you cut section A 20¾" long and section C 11¾" long which is allowing for seams and a 1" hem. This is for a 31" long skirt. You can increase or decrease the length of tiers to any required length. Sections A front and back should be cut wider at the bottom than top, the top sections should each be 9" wider than half the waist measurement and the bottom of this section should each be 21" wider than half the waist measurement. Section C should be cut 38" wider than half the waist measurement, top and bottom to be the same.

You now cut your waist band and proceed to make in the same way as your two tiered skirt. You should now be able to make a skirt with any number of tiers you wish by following these instructions. Quantity of material required when using a 60" wide material is twice the length of your skirt plus seam and hem allowances. In this instance 2 yards for either of these skirts would be correct.

You may have some short lengths of materials put by from previous sewing that you have made, by utilising them, you should be able to make one of these skirts, as contrasting tiers will look quite attractive.

Tiered Skirts

2   3   1

150

Tiered Skirts

The Tabard

Diag 100

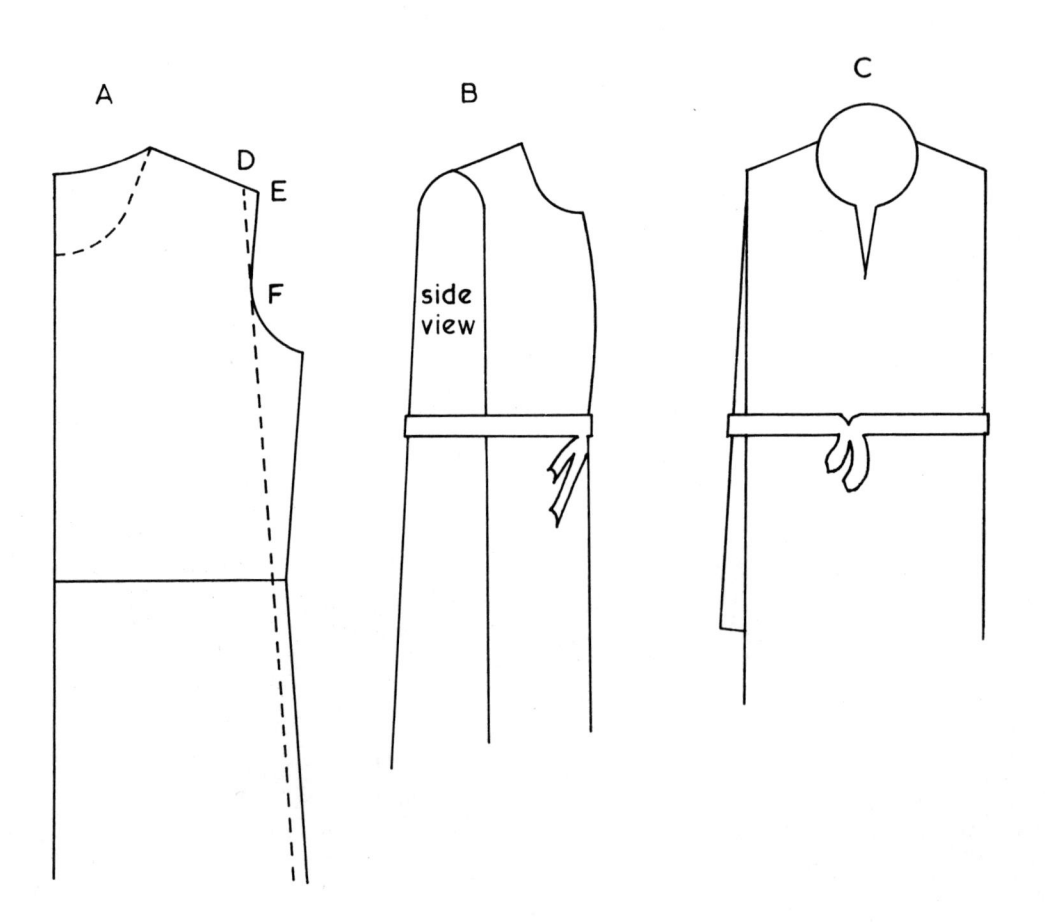

A   B   C

D
E
F

side view

fiftysix

The Tabard

This is a loose fitting garment usually worn over a blouse, jumper, skirt or slacks. Diagram 100 B and C are front and side views of one of many styles that can be made. Some are made with a tie belt others with side straps. This is done to hold the garment in position when worn, as side seams are not sewn together. There is no shaping required for a tabard which consists of two pieces of material only sewn at the shoulders. The side seams and neck are either bound with the same or contrasting material, or simply turned back and sewn either by hand or machine and the bottom turned up and sewn.

The average length worn is about hip length, but there is no hard or fast rule, it is a matter of one's own choice. The neck shape can be either round, squared or any other shape you like. Some of these garments are even made without shoulder seams simply by using one piece of material folded in halves at the top. This should be a piece of material double the length of garment plus allowance for hem at bottom.

Diagram 100 A shows how the garment can be cut. As there are no front or back seams in your tabard, you must lay your block pattern on the material with the centre front and centre back onto the fold of material. If using a 36" wide material and your hip measurement is over 38" you will require double the length of garment plus hem allowance. If hip measurement is less than 38" one length plus hem allowance should be enough.

Once you have marked out your garment by using your block pattern you run a line from D diagram 100 A which is 1" from E. This is run straight down touching at armhole at F to the bottom of garment, which you will note does not reach to your material hip width, this is correct as this garment is open at the sides. This is done on both front and back sections of garment. Now proceed to shape neck and cut either your tie belt or side straps. The garment is now ready for sewing.

This is quite an easy and very useful garment to make, and should not take up too much of your spare time.

The Pinafore Dress

Diag 101

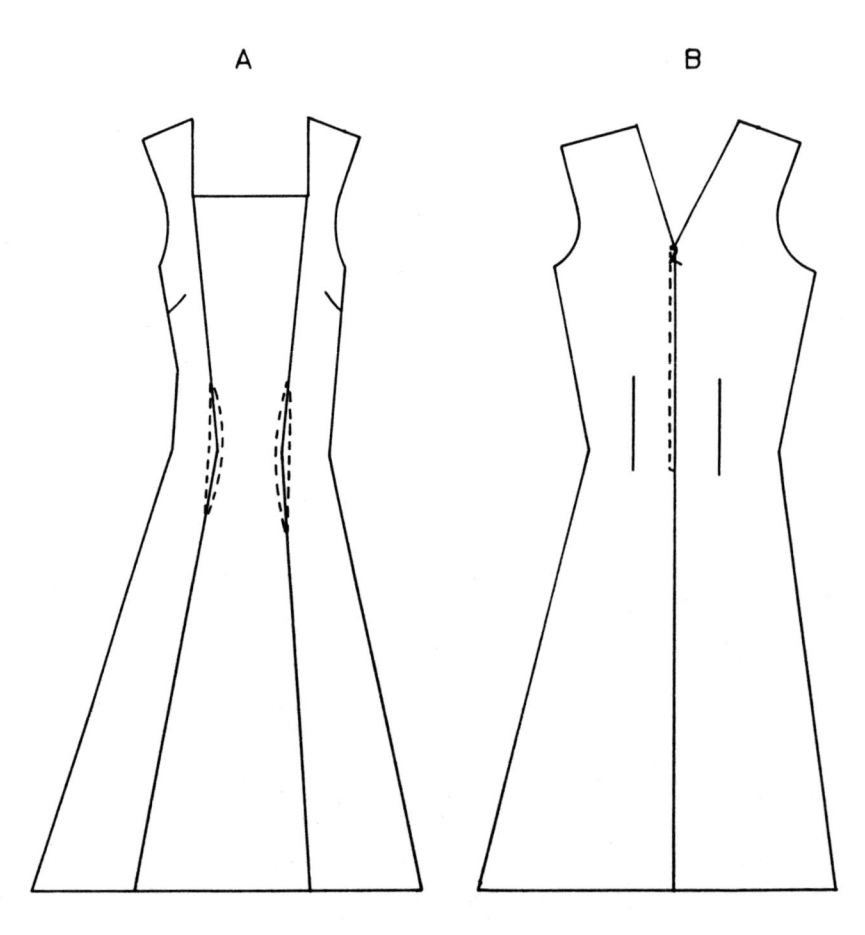

A B

fiftyseven

The Pinafore Dress

Here is a basic pattern for a pinafore dress. You can see how, by using one's own creative imagination, how many different styles can be made by using the same pattern. Diagram 101 style A is a square cut neck with a slight flair at the bottom of the dress with front seams coming down from the neck line. Underarm darts are provided to give shape over bust. Broken lines in front indicate where suppression can be increased or decreased to required shaping. As back and front styles of this dress are both the same you only require a front block and this is used to cut the back of the dress as well as the front — the only difference being that you do not cut underarm darts at the back.

Mark your design onto your block diagram 102a as broken lines indicate. Now cut through broken lines and lay your pattern onto your material as diagram 102b. Broken lines on diagram b are allowances marked out onto your material, these are 3/8" from top down to waist. This is to allow for seams, then come out to 3" or 4" at the bottom depending on how wide you want the flair to be.

Both C and D are allowances for your underarm darts approximately 1½". This should only be added when cutting the dress fronts as there are no darts at the back. Depth of neck is approximately 7" but can be lowered as you wish.

Diagram 102b is a V neck with both back and front cut the same, therefore your front or back block is the only one required. There are both back and front darts to this dress. These should not be cut through but pinned up when fitting your garment for correct positioning.

Your normal block is laid onto your material and you allow 3/8" centre front and back for seams which extend from centre of neck to bottom of dress. Should you require a zip down the front, you then allow 1" for sewing zip onto instead of 3/8". Depth of neck line is a matter of your own choice. This can be cut 7" down for fitting and then lowered accordingly. These garments are worn over a blouse or jumper, usually with long sleeves, therefore no sleeves are required for a pinafore dress.

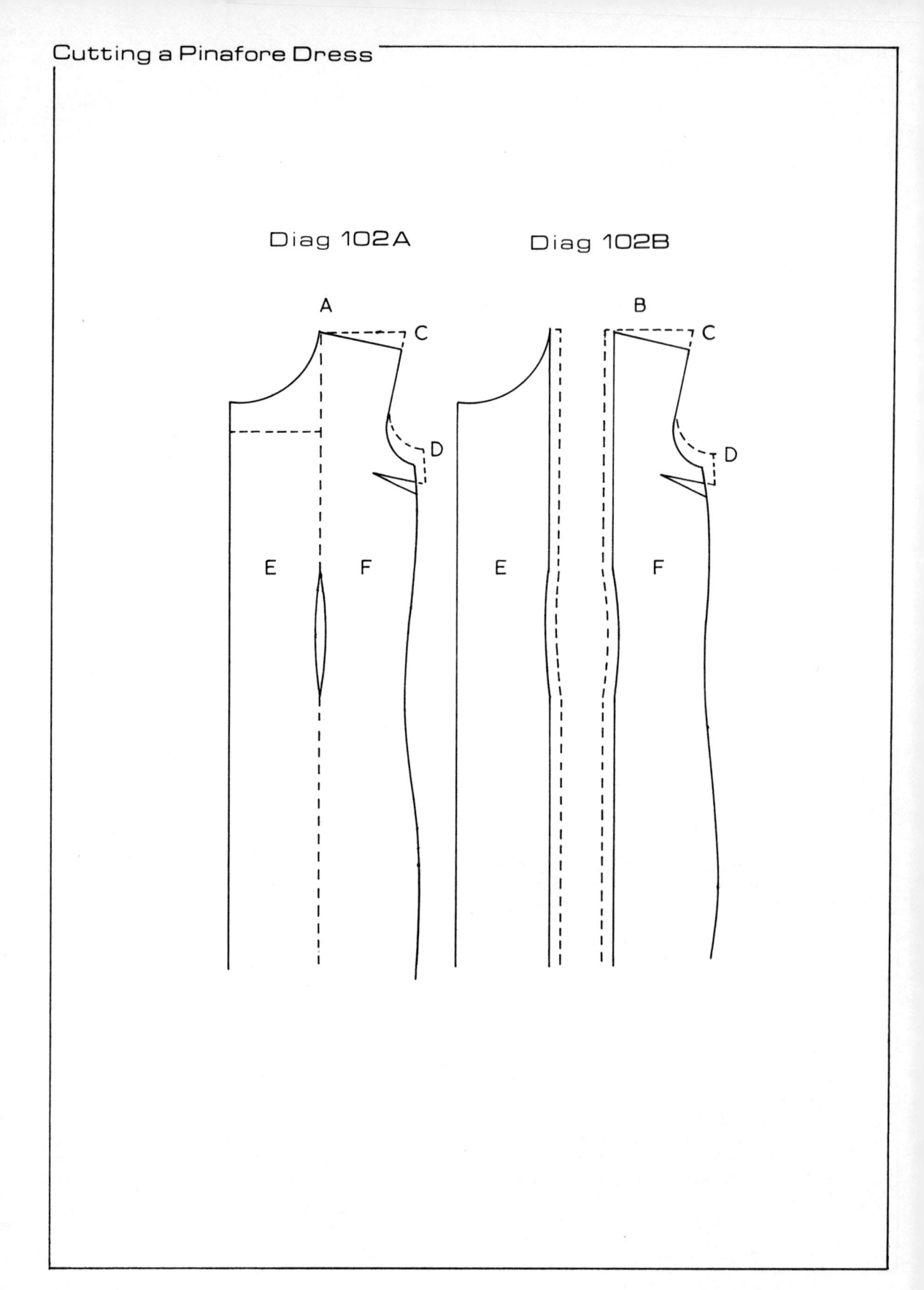

Cutting a Pinafore Dress

Diag 102A

Diag 102B

Pinafore Dresses

Pinafore Dresses

1

2

158

Pinafore Dresses

Over Dress

Diag 103

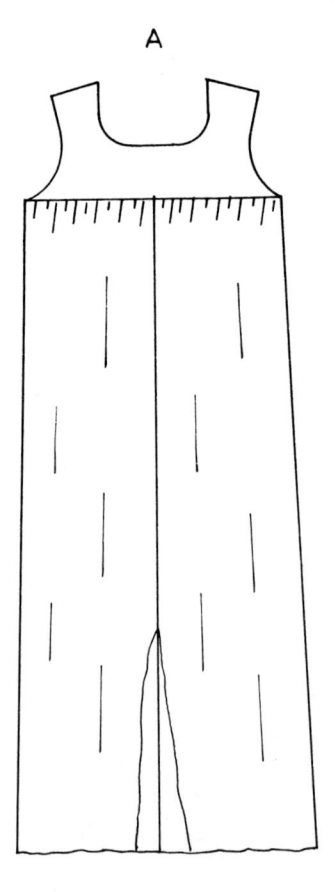

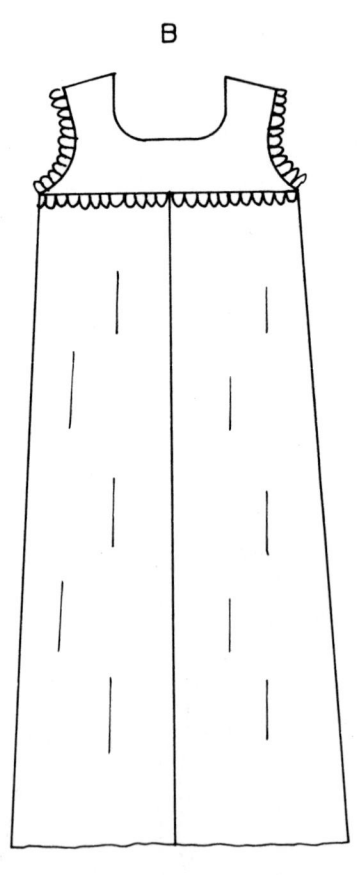

A B

fiftyeight

Over Dress

Like the pinafore dress this is worn over a jumper or blouse and is a loose fitting garment without sleeves. Measurements required are your length, bust and hip, there is no shaping at the waist.

To cut this dress you require both back and front block patterns. Diagram 104 section A is back block pattern with yolk marked onto it. Cut through yolk and place onto material as diagram 104 section B indicates. Broken lines are $3/8$ " seam allowances for yolk, and 1" at centre back for sewing zip onto. Broken lines at side seams are 4" allowances for gathering onto yolk. Diagram 104 section C is front block pattern. Yolk should be marked onto this, front of yolk being ¾" lower than at side seam to allow for bust lift. Diagram 104 section D is the front pattern cut through at yolk and laid onto the material, broken lines are seam allowances and 4" allowance at side seams for gathering onto yolk. As there is no seam in the centre front of yolk this section should be cut on fold of material. The neck line can be cut to your own choice, usually about 7" down from neck point. I have suggested 4" allowances at side seams for gathering, this can be altered to any desired amount you wish to have gathered in. The skirt section from below the yolk can be cut on the cross of the material to give a nice swing to your garment.

Diagram 103B is the same dress with lace trimming around neck and yolk. Your dress is now ready for basting and fitting before finishing. Styles can be varied to your own choice the principle always being the same by drawing your design lines on to your block pattern and always allow $3/8$ " for seams when cutting your design sections.

Over Dress

Diag 103C

A
B
C

Over Dress

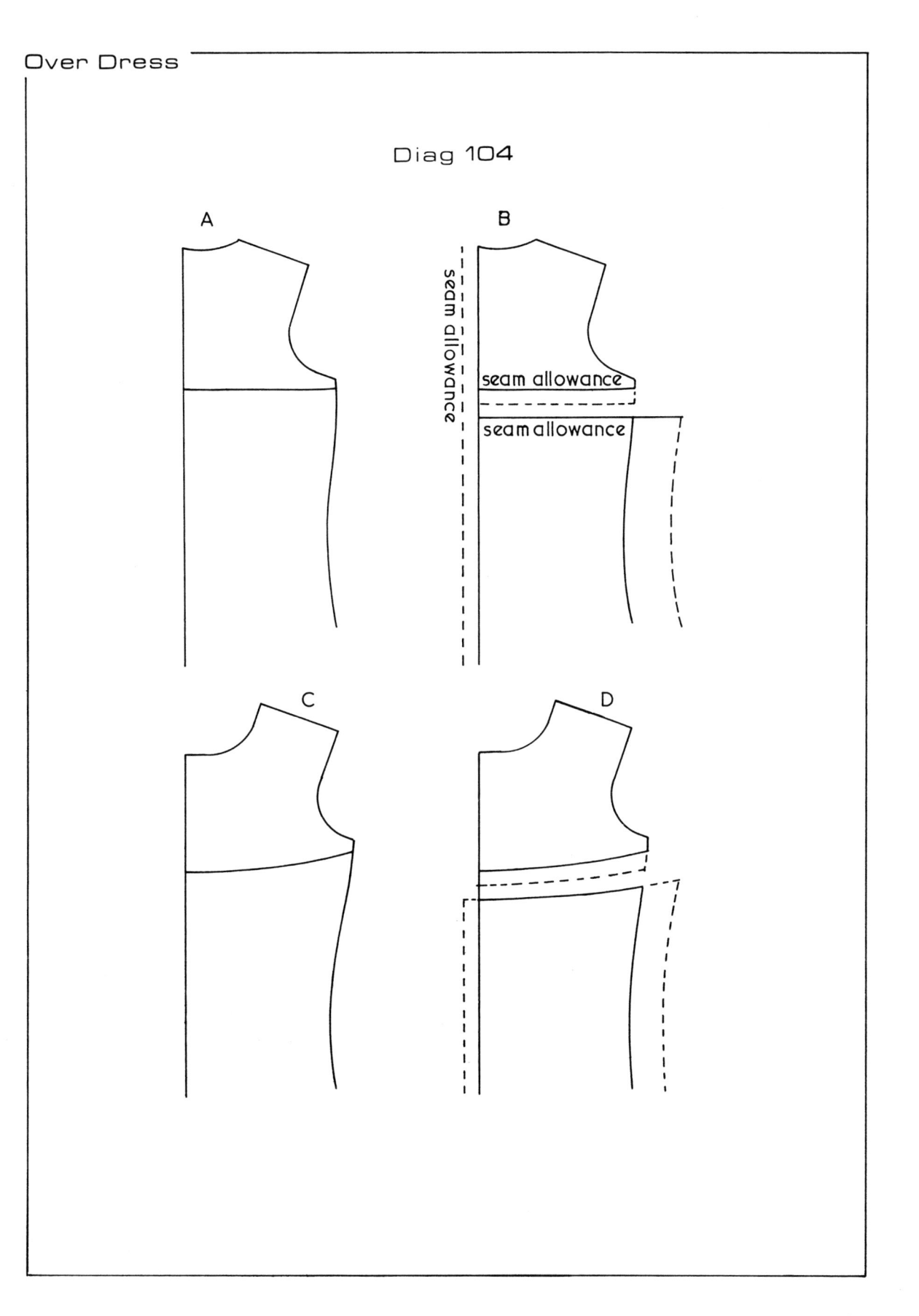

Diag 104

A

B

seam allowance

seam allowance

seam allowance

C

D

Smocked Tops

Diag 105

A

B

fiftynine

Smocked Tops

Smocked tops are loose and flowing usually with gathering around the neck and sleeve head and sleeves, or even cut with a raglan sleeve. You may choose a button front or a closed front with neck opening only, the choice is up to the reader.

Starting with Diagram 105 style A this is cut with an elbow length gathered sleeve, button front and turn back collar. When cutting your pattern you should add 2" to your normal bust and hip measurements to allow for ease, waist measurements are not required as side seams are cut straight from bust down to hip line, length is approximately to the hip line. Your pattern should be cut by following instructions on Page 14 diagram 2 using your own measurements. Diagram 107 shows block pattern of back and front with allowances for gathering and button wrap at fronts. Broken line at front A is 2" for wrap, broken lines above 3, back and front are 1¼" allowances for gathering around neck.

Collar is cut by following instructions on Collars Page 31 diagram 11. You require a single piece of material cut on the cross of the material. This should measure the same distance as your neck from A to 3 and from B on to 3 of back, and the width should be approximately 6". Fold your collar in halves and round off ends at folded double edge, the raw edge is sewn on to the garment. Diagram 107 also shows collar opened out when cut and also when folded over with ends rounded off.

Sleeves are cut by following instructions on Pages 16 and 17 Diagram 3B.

To make your first fold back the front facings at A 1", this leaves 1" for sewing your buttons on to, also for making button holes on right hand side of front. You now baste your side seams and shoulders and draw in your neck with a running stitch around the back and fronts as diagram 105 shows. Sew the rounded parts of collar and baste on to your blouse. Sleeves should now be basted in, easing in over shoulders and gathered at elbows. After making any adjustments that may be required your garment should now be ready for finishing and making button holes which should be made ¾" from front edge.

Diagram 105B is cut slightly differently. As there are no button holes you only allow ⅜" on fronts for seam with opening at the top approximately 7" down from the neck point at 3. The sleeves are full length and gathered with a narrow band at the cuff. There is also a cord of the same material sewn on under the collar which can be worn tied at the neck. Diagram 106 shows other styles that can be made with a raglan sleeve. These are cut by following instructions on Pages 50 and 51 Diagram 25. Do not cut off section C to D on diagram 23 Page 50, this should be cut at A down to C to allow for gathering. For this style of garment it is better to baste sleeve in before gathering around the neck, the rest of the blouse is now made in the same way as diagram 105. Garments in these styles can also be cut as full length dresses.

Smocked Tops

Diag 106

Smocked Tops

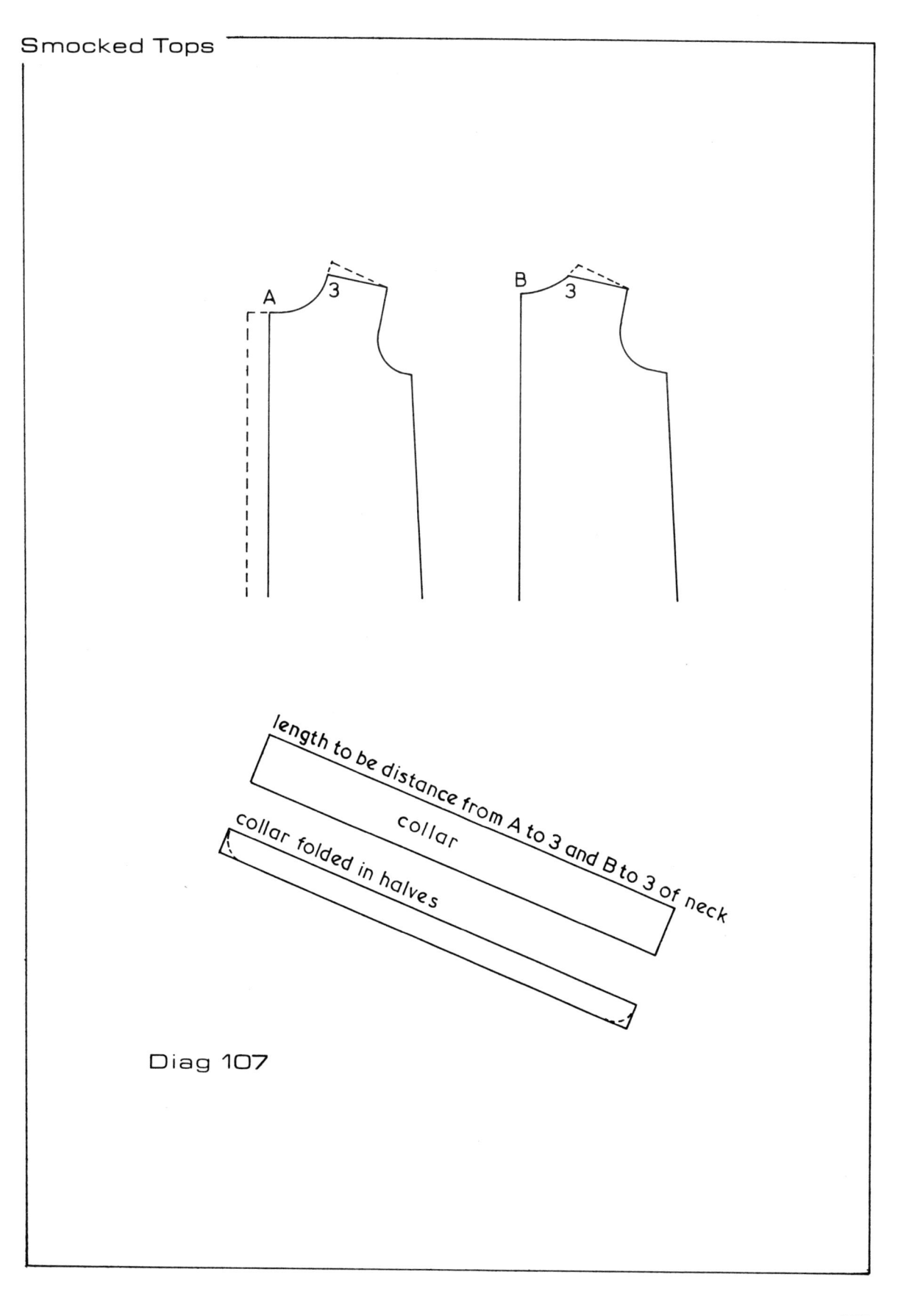

length to be distance from A to 3 and B to 3 of neck
collar
collar folded in halves

Diag 107

Cutting Velvet or Materials with a pile

When cutting a velvet material always be certain that the pile is going upwards. By rubbing the palm of your hands over your material you can tell which way the pile is going, it should feel smooth when you rub your hands upwards and rough when rubbing your hands downwards. Every section of your garment must be cut in the same direction otherwise your material will look a different shade and is liable to wear out in some places sooner than others.

When using any other material with a pile or knap, this should be cut the reverse way with pile or knap going downwards. When rubbing the palm of your hand downwards on material it should feel smooth. Cut every section with the pile going downwards. This is very important to the finished appearance of the garment.